Praise for *Fire and Ice*

"Michael Adams accurately describes the value structure beneath the current Canadian-American debate." —*The Globe and Mail*

"Impressive evidence in support of sweeping and profound conclusions about the people of Canada and the United States." —*Edmonton Journal*

"If timing is everything, Toronto pollster Michael Adams clocks in perfectly with his latest book . . . *Fire and Ice* is a good read that would appeal to anyone who has an interest in social values in general and the differences between Canadian and American societies in particular."
—*Winnipeg Free Press*

"Persuasive and arresting . . ." —*Toronto Star*

"The timing of the book couldn't be better, given that Canadian angst over our differences has translated into a parade of cabinet ministers heading for Washington to smooth the waters with the U.S. on things like missile defence and marijuana use." —*The Gazette* (Montreal)

"Adams makes a powerful argument that Canadians and Americans are motivated by very different value systems and that these differences have become more marked in recent years." —*The Daily News* (Halifax)

"Thoroughly engaging . . ." —*National Post*

"Michael Adams . . . gives an intriguing snapshot of Canada and the U.S. at the beginning of the New Millennium." —*Ottawa Citizen*

"[Adams'] findings titillate because they fly in the face of conventional wisdom; namely, that the two similar societies, inundated by the same brain-numbing, body-bloating doses of American reality TV and fast food, will grow more and more alike over time, turning Canadians into 'unarmed Americans with health insurance,' as they like to say up north."
—*Seattle Times*

Praise for *Sex in the Snow*

"*Sex in the Snow* is a serious and intriguing analysis of a nation and society in transition."   —*Maclean's*

"Adams's book has much to offer. It is a useful corrective to the determinism of popular demography."   —*The Globe and Mail*

"[Adams's] provocative statements are worth considering . . . The fun in reading *Sex in the Snow* is in trying to decide which tribe is yours . . . We see ourselves in a mirror—and the reflection prompts us to think about who is behind the face staring back."   —*The Daily News* (Halifax)

"Thought-provoking and fun . . . challenging and original."
—*Calgary Herald*

"[*Sex in the Snow*] portrays citizens' diversity. Based on in-depth surveys of our social values and scientific investigations of the underlying motivations that propel our culture, it reveals the evolution of the Canadian character and forecasts our future directions."   —*Northern Daily News*
(Kirkland Lake, Ontario)

"An overview of changing Canadian society . . . a new original look into the souls of Canadians. Adams's work gives a new and sometimes startling picture of Canadians . . . *Sex in the Snow* is engagingly written."
—*The Leader-Post* (Regina)

"[Adams] is on target when he discusses the diminishment of established authority and the rise of the priority of choice in all spheres of life. He also helps us understand what might be behind Ontario's sudden swing to the political right."   —*The Record* (Kitchener-Waterloo)

PENGUIN CANADA

FIRE AND ICE

Michael Adams is the president of the Environics group of research and communications consulting companies with offices in Toronto, Montreal, Calgary, Ottawa, New York, and Washington. Outside the field of research consulting, Adams has a variety of other interests, including a partnership in a Napa Valley winery. He is the author of *Better Happy Than Rich? Canadians, Money and the Meaning of Life* and the bestselling *Sex in the Snow: Canadian Social Values at the End of the Millennium*. He and his partner, Donna Dasko, vice president of Environics, have two children.

Also by Michael Adams

*Sex in the Snow: Canadian Social Values
at the End of the Millennium*

*Better Happy Than Rich?
Canadians, Money and the Meaning of Life*

FIRE AND ICE

THE UNITED STATES, CANADA AND THE MYTH OF CONVERGING VALUES

MICHAEL ADAMS

with Amy Langstaff and David Jamieson

PENGUIN
CANADA

PENGUIN CANADA

Penguin Group (Canada), a division of Pearson Penguin Canada Inc.,
10 Alcorn Avenue, Toronto, Ontario M4V 3B2

Penguin Group (U.K.), 80 Strand, London WC2R 0RL, England
Penguin Group (U.S.), 375 Hudson Street, New York, New York 10014, U.S.A.
Penguin Group (Australia) Inc., 250 Camberwell Road, Camberwell, Victoria 3124, Australia
Penguin Group (Ireland), 25 St. Stephen's Green, Dublin 2, Ireland
Penguin Books India (P) Ltd, 11, Community Centre, Panchsheel Park, New Delhi – 110 017, India
Penguin Group (NZ), cnr Airborne and Rosedale Roads, Albany, Auckland 1310, New Zealand
Penguin Books (South Africa) (Pty) Ltd, 24 Sturdee Avenue, Rosebank 2196, South Africa

Penguin Group, Registered Offices: 80 Strand, London WC2R 0RL, England

First published in Penguin Canada hardcover by Penguin Group (Canada),
a division of Pearson Penguin Canada Inc., 2003
Published in this edition, 2004

2 3 4 5 6 7 8 9 10   (WEB)

Author representation: Westwood Creative Artists
94 Harbord Street, Toronto, Ontario M5S 1G6

The cartoons on pages 3, 19, 56, 60, 69, 99, 109 and 142 are
copyright © *The New Yorker* magazine. They are reprinted with permission.

Manufactured in Canada.

NATIONAL LIBRARY OF CANADA CATALOGUING IN PUBLICATION

Adams, Michael, 1946 Sept. 29–
Fire and ice : United States, Canada and the myth of converging values / Michael Adams.

Includes bibliographical references and index.
ISBN 0-14-301422-6 (bound).—ISBN 0-14-301423-4 (pbk.)

1. Canada—Relations—United States. 2. United States—Relations—Canada.
3. Social values—Canada. 4. National characteristics, Canadian. 5. Social values—United States.
6. National characteristics, American. I. Title.

FC249.A33 2003   303.48'271073   C2003-901510-6
F1029.5.U6A33 2003

Visit the Penguin Group (Canada) website at **www.penguin.ca**

For Donna Dasko, Marion Adams, and William Adams

CONTENTS

PREFACE

M Y FASCINATION WITH THE UNITED STATES started with Elvis
Presley's appearances on *The Ed Sullivan Show* in the mid-1950s and crys-
tallized with the 1960 presidential campaign and election of John F.
Kennedy. One could say that the research for this book began that same
year, when at the age of fourteen I put my Roman Catholic catechism on
the shelf and started my subscription to *Time* magazine.

My interest in Canada and its politics did not begin in earnest until I
went off to Queen's University in Kingston in 1965 to study political
science and join the Progressive Conservative club on campus. I signed
up with the Tories in defiance of a family tradition established by my
great-grandfather, who had won election to both federal and provincial
parliaments as a "Clear Grit" Liberal from Bruce County in Western
Ontario. I felt the Conservatives were more likely than the other parties
to assert Canadian sovereignty after reading philosopher George Grant's
Lament for a Nation, a nationalist anti-American diatribe.

My interest in the United States was rekindled in university, first at
Queen's and subsequently at the University of Toronto, when my political science and sociology courses exposed me to the research of American
social scientist Seymour Martin Lipset, who had written intriguing books
about the political cultures of our two countries. I have maintained an
avid interest in the work of Lipset and other cross-cultural sociologists
ever since.

I remained active in party politics for a number of years, but faded into
non-partisanship when the firm I had co-founded, Environics, began
conducting and publishing polls for *The Globe and Mail* in the early
1980s. By the late 1980s my intellectual interest had shifted from public
opinion polling to market research and the impact of social values on

consumer marketing, public affairs, and human resources, first in Canada, then in the United States, and today in many parts of the world where my firm has expanded its scope.

My first book, *Sex in the Snow: Canadian Social Values at the End of the Millennium,* published in 1997, describes the evolution of social values in Canada in the last half-century and segments the country into twelve social values tribes. But when I first began looking seriously at the data that would culminate in the publication of *Sex in the Snow,* I was interested in more than just the story of social change within our own borders. I was also impressed with just how much Canadians' social values seemed to be diverging from those of Americans. (After all, we are frequently made to feel that we have become nothing more than unarmed Americans with health insurance.) That was in 1996–97. By the time the Environics' team of statistical wizards had analyzed the data from our year 2000 surveys in the two countries, I knew a truly fascinating and important story had emerged: a tale of two *(yes, two)* nations. The divergence that was interesting when we first apprehended it in 1992, and surprisingly strong when we measured it again in 1996, had become by 2000 a remarkably wide and growing gap. The respective social values trajectories of the societies on either side of the 49th parallel revealed a story that turned a great deal of talk of Canada–U.S. cultural convergence on its head. I was eager to take a closer look and to let Canadians know about these surprising findings.

Simone de Beauvoir wrote in her introduction to *The Second Sex* that she had long hesitated to write the book because "Enough ink has been spilled in quarrelling over feminism, now practically over, and perhaps we should say no more about it." That was in 1949. Beauvoir's book (she did manage to spill enough additional ink to fill 700 pages or so) effectively launched the feminist movement as we have known it in the second half of the twentieth century. I think it's safe to say that I have a sense of the apprehension Beauvoir felt; a massive amount has already been written on the subject of Canada vis-à-vis its behemoth neighbour—the subject has been our national obsession at least since the War of 1812, and probably longer. But the increasingly interesting and counterintuitive story that our socio-cultural data have told during the past decade has convinced me that much of value remains to be said on the subject.

We live in an era when everything must be measured—U.S. sociologist Ben Wattenberg and his colleagues term the twentieth century the "first measured century." But those measures were too often body counts in wars and disasters, and lately too often economic statistics of quarters of growth or decline of our gross domestic product or, increasingly, the ups and downs of the world's stock markets. We have no equivalent measures of life's quality or metrics of the human spirit. It's as if we see ourselves and those in the rest of the world only through the prism of fear and greed.

The goal in our research is to broaden that lens and add colour and texture to the stark black and white portraits we are exposed to every day in the media. Our goal is to bring to the "real world" some truths that are normally the province of art, music, and fiction. But like the economists and demographers, we too have our measures, however crude and imperfect, of human values.

Our results will be obvious to some, but will surprise many, and, I hope, will be of interest not just to Canadians but to others who feel overwhelmed by the globalization of American commerce and popular culture. Indeed, I also dream it might even find an audience in the United States.

Fire and Ice is the story I have been wishing to tell for a very long time.

ACKNOWLEDGEMENTS

This book is the result of two years of analysis, thinking, debating, reading, and writing by a remarkable team of social researchers. Data analysis was led by David Jamieson, Ph.D., Environics' chief scientist and head of our Advanced Analytics department, and his colleagues Kevin Shanahan, Dennis Maslo, and Lee Francis. Guiding our internal workshops was David MacDonald, who heads Environics' global automotive and market research practice, and his colleague Joanne Di Maio. David Jamieson and David MacDonald, under the leadership of Environics Research Group's president, Barry Watson, are collectively responsible for the incredible amount of socio-cultural research and development work behind the collection and analysis of the unique data set in the Environics archive that is the basis of this book.

Working closely with me in crafting words that expressed our findings and putting them into larger socio-historical context was my brilliant young colleague Amy Langstaff. Amy and I are both deeply grateful to our administrative assistants Karen Hume and Erica Cerny. My colleague Chris Baker, who heads up Environics' public affairs practice in Ottawa, read an early manuscript and provided a number of useful comments.

I want to thank my friends Murray Barkley and Janet Noel for helping me clarify the historical facts and their interpretation cited in Chapter Four and to acknowledge my intellectual debt to Alain de Vulpian, who pioneered our socio-cultural tradition in France in the 1970s. I also wish to express my gratitude to two friends and colleagues, Alain Giguere, the president of CROP in Montreal, whose firm conducts the annual socio-cultural program in Canada, and Larry Kaagan, the president of his own research company in New York, who provided me with very useful and at times chastening feedback on an earlier draft of this book. Alain and Larry worked with me in the early 1990s in devising our first social values questionnaire in the United States and analyzing and interpreting our early results. They, I hope, will be pleased with this book, wondering of course why it took me so long.

This book, like everything Environics ever does, is a collective effort. However, it would not have happened without the negotiating skills of my polymath agent Bruce Westwood and the continuing and enthusiastic support of my formidable publisher Cynthia Good, both of whom encouraged me to put this remarkable story into words.

And finally, it seems appropriate to thank not only those whose work has contributed directly to the creation of this work, but also those whose example has given life to this entire brand of endeavour. I have been inspired by many curious and thoughtful people who have sought to understand whole societies: sociologists, economists, political thinkers, and journalists. Those who have been drawn to study Canada are of particular interest to me, and as I have written this book I have often thought of the projects and legacies of Canadian authors Pierre Berton and Peter C. Newman and CBC producer Mark Starowicz. If, in their tradition of speaking to wider audiences and telling stories of Canada that might not otherwise have been told, I can offer my fellow Canadians some new insight into this country and its character, I will be well satisfied.

INTRODUCTION

I don't even know what street Canada is on.
—Al "Scarface" Capone

While Americans are benevolently ignorant about Canada,
most Canadians seem malevolently informed about the United States.
—Merrill Denison, "4,000 Miles of Irritation,"
Saturday Review of Literature, 7 June 1952

The Americans are our best friends, whether we like it or not.
—Robert Thompson, national leader of the Social Credit Party (1961–1967),
quoted by Peter C. Newman in *Home Country,* 1973

THE WORLD HAS LONG WATCHED the United States with a mixture of envy, admiration, resentment, fear, and disgust. Perhaps nowhere are these feelings more potent—or the watching more constant—than in Canada. We are under no illusions about our neighbour's accomplishments: America is the economic engine of Western capitalism; it is the source of astounding technological innovation; it is the matrix of popular culture; it is a military power like no other in history.

We take pains to remind ourselves, too, though, that America's crime rates in all categories are triple those in other industrialized nations; that its carnivalesque displays of wealth cannot conceal the rage and despair of its poorest; that Canada strives to be an upstanding citizen of the world while the United States has, under George W. Bush, reaffirmed its commitment to brash unilateralism; that Canada consistently outranks the U.S. in the United Nations' Human Development Index, the planet's de facto annual quality-of-life ranking.

It is perhaps this last difference in which Canadians take the greatest comfort: on a personal level, Canadians sense that although Americans may make the more impressive living, Canadians have better gotten the hang of how to live. Looking south, we feel that even many of those who are ostensibly successful seem unable to savour their success, to enjoy the happiness promised in Thomas Jefferson's Declaration of Independence. And as the temporary cohesion engendered by the tragedies of 11 September continues to weaken, Americans seem to be returning to business as usual—lives that appear (from above) relentlessly competitive, perilously chaotic, perennially unfulfilling.

For all of our pressing our noses up against the glass of American prosperity and achievement, we cherish our separateness—our unassuming civility, our gift for irony and understatement in a world of exaggerated claims and excess, the myriad "intangibles" we are certain set us apart—and wring our hands over what will become of our quirks and idiosyncrasies as the leviathan to the south continues to thrash its ever more powerful tail and the self-declared prophets of globalization augur the death of difference.

This book is about Canadians and Americans. It offers up the results of the pulse-taking that Environics has been performing on both sides of the border during the past decade and elaborates, through the lens of social change, the national histories that have brought Canadians to their current uneasy coexistence with their Yankee neighbours. It discusses the trajectories the two societies seem to be following—trajectories that, contrary to Jeffrey Simpson's views in his book *Star-Spangled Canadians*[1] and echoed by Michael Bliss in a January 2003 series of articles in the *National Post*[2]

---

1. Simpson writes, "Canadians, whether they like or acknowledge it, have never been more like Americans, and Canadian society has never been more similar to that of the United States. If the two countries are becoming more alike, and they are, this drawing together does not arise because Americans are changing. Canadians are the ones whose habits of mind, cultural preferences, economy, and political choices are becoming more American—without being American" (p. 6).

2. In a dialogue with *National Post* features writer Brian Hutchinson, University of Toronto historian and author Michael Bliss is quoted as saying: "But what strikes me is that we are becoming more similar to the Americans in our culture and in our values" (*National Post*, 18 January 2003, p. B1).

on the evolving Canadian identity, are not ineluctably drawing together but actually diverging in subtle but important ways.

To be fair, Simpson and Bliss are certainly not alone in their belief that Canada and the United States are becoming more similar. When Ekos Research asked Canadians in May 2002 whether they thought Canada had been becoming more or less similar to the United States during the preceding ten years, a majority of respondents (58 per cent) replied that they thought Canada was becoming more American. Thirty-one per cent thought there had been no change in the two countries' similarity or difference, and a mere 9 per cent thought Canada was becoming increasingly distinct from the United States. When asked whether they wanted Canada to be more like or less like the U.S., a majority of Canadians (52 per cent) reported that they would like Canada to be less like its neighbour. Thirty-four percent wanted the two countries' identities and relationship to remain the way they are now, and only 12 per cent of Canadians desired greater convergence with the U.S.

"I hate getting all these Canadian coins, but I guess that's the price of living in Toronto."

In this book I advance the rarely heard, and even more rarely substantiated, thesis that Canadians and Americans are actually becoming increasingly different from one another. Canadians are everywhere confronted with the claim that our southern border is rapidly becoming irrelevant: our health care system will soon cease to differentiate us as a nation; our beloved Queen Elizabeth will not be able to hold out much longer against George Washington on the battleground of international currency; we may have to hand the controls of our immigration and refugee systems over to Uncle Sam in the name of continental security; and our ongoing gobbling of American media and popular culture will soon endanger any differences that may yet linger even in our very minds. The left chants these supposed omens of convergence in grave tones, while the right brightly trumpets them as signs that rational markets are at last poised to triumph over the illogic of national borders. What I propose to show in the following pages is that the rarely disputed prognosis of Canada–U.S. cultural convergence is, in important ways, false. At the most basic level—the level of our values, the feelings and beliefs that inform our understanding of and interaction with the world around us—Canadians and Americans are markedly different, and are becoming more so.

The claims I make and the conclusions I reach are at their core based on scientific surveys of representative samples of Americans and Canadians conducted during the past decade. The analytic tool I use in this book is the same as that which produced the 1997 Canadian bestseller, *Sex in the Snow: Canadian Social Values at the End of the Millennium*. The success of *Sex in the Snow* proves not only that there is a market in Canada for serious books about social values, but also that social values research produces insights into individuals and groups that resonate with and intrigue Canadians. Canadians were interested in *Sex in the Snow,* which divides Canadian society into segments, or "tribes," based on their social values. It is my hope that readers will be even more interested in this social values–based analysis, which focuses, this time, not on the differences among Canadians, but on the characteristics that differentiate Canadians from Americans.

In 1867, Canada's Fathers of Confederation dedicated this country to "peace, order, and good government" while the ideals set out in Thomas Jefferson's Declaration of Independence were "life, liberty, and the pursuit of happiness." Americans were the revolutionaries putting in place institutions designed to frustrate the authority of governments, while counterrevolutionary Canadians saw the authority of political institutions as central to the well-being of their country. America has long honoured the individual fighting for truth and justice; Canadians have tended to defer to elites who broker compromises between groups. The American motto is *E Pluribus Unum,* Out of Many, One. In Canada, we began as two founding European cultures, French and English, since officially expanded to a multiculturalism that includes not only more recent immigrants, but also the First Nations that were here long before Europeans arrived. The Americans separated Church and State; we entrenched state sponsorship of parochial education in our Constitution. Canada never having renounced its European political heritage (at least not as emphatically as the American revolutionaries did), the Old World ideal of noblesse oblige has survived here even into this century, informing our social assistance and public housing programs, while south of the border mass education in the service of individual achievement has been the primary public expenditure. From distinct roots, Canada and the U.S. have grown up with substantially different characters: group rights, public institutions, and deference to authority have abided north of the border, while individualism, private interests, and mistrust of authority have remained strong to the south.

But in the last quarter-century, some counterintuitive developments have occurred on both sides of the 49th parallel. Canadians have distanced themselves from traditional authority: organized religion, the patriarchal family, and political elites. Peter C. Newman has characterized recent social change in Canada as the movement from deference to defiance. Meanwhile, a greater proportion of Americans are clinging to old institutions—family, church, state, and myriad clubs, voluntary associations, even gangs—as anchors in a chaotic world. In a country where the price of untrammelled individualism is that, in an instant, illness, crime, or an injudicious investment portfolio can turn the Dream into a nightmare, many Americans are seeking refuge at church, with family, or in the gated communities that are now, according to the Community Associations Institute as quoted in the 30 August 2001 edition of *The Economist,* home to a sixth of the U.S. population. In many ways, it is Canadians who have become the true revolutionaries, at least when it comes to social life. In fact, it has become apparent to me that Canadians are at the forefront of a fascinating and important social experiment: we are coming to define a new sociological "postmodernity" characterized by multiple, flexible roles and identities while Americans, weaned for generations on ideals of freedom and independence, have in general not found adequate security and stability in their social environment to allow them to assert the personal autonomy needed to enact the kind of individual explorations— spiritual, familial, sexual—that are taking place north of the border.

THIS IS A BOOK ABOUT VALUES, the basic learned motivators of human behaviour. While we come into the world with genetically coded instincts common to all human beings, such as the sex drive, our culture has an overwhelming influence on what we come to value in life. Historically, the most powerful values humans come to learn are religious values. Anthropologists spend their lives finding out what people grasped for in the past. Sociologists focus on what we aspire to today. Each tries to find out why we value what we do and what patterns of values are common to all known cultures or only a few or even one.

I have academic training in many of the social sciences, but my career has been that of a pollster who is perpetually doing soundings of public opinion on politics and public policy or surveys on attitudes toward consumer products and services. Polling is to sociology what the daily news is to history. It can take years of research before the pollster sees the emergence of meaningful patterns; in my case, it took me a quarter of a century to muster the courage to articulate the convictions of my survey respondents.

People in modern cultures like Canada and the United States have opinions on almost every subject, even in the absence of much specific knowledge on the topic being probed. This is because most of us are literate and well educated and reasonably aware of the world around us. We also share with other "moderns" a quality indispensable to pollsters and market researchers: we are expressive—willing, if not always eager, to tell others what we think.

Like Blanche DuBois in Tennessee Williams's *A Streetcar Named Desire,* we pollsters rely upon the kindness of strangers. Not so long ago, a Canadian approached by a pollster would have replied, "It's none of your business." My grandmother might have said, "You'll have to speak to my husband." In Iran and many other parts of the world today, a pollster cannot talk to a woman without her husband's permission. Here in Canada, and perhaps even more so in the United States, everyone has an opinion on the world around them, often very strongly held, and no adult (who is not in prison) needs anyone's permission to express it.

During the 1970s and 1980s, it became apparent to me that people's loyalties to political parties, as well as to brands of consumer products and the companies who made them, were beginning to erode. Canadians no longer voted for the political party their family had always supported and they no longer bought the same car that Dad had replaced every three or four years. In fact, one generation, the Baby Boomers—born between 1946–47 and 1964–66 and brought up during a time of peace and affluence—were taught to think for themselves and to question authority, and did so in droves, many even rejecting almost all forms of traditional authority, practice, and proper behaviour. We had, in the words of political scientist Neil Nevitte, become agents in the "decline of deference."

This evolution from adherence to traditional authority to individual autonomy in Canada was evidence that more was going on in the culture than a change of attachment to political parties and their leaders or to preferences among manufacturers and their brands. Something deeper was happening: our fundamental values, motivations, and mindsets were changing. We did not see life and its possibilities the way our parents and grandparents had.

Over time it became apparent to me that many of the values that were in flux were correlated or associated with each other. People who questioned the norm of patriarchal authority in the family were very often the same people who questioned the words the priest or minister had delivered from the pulpit. They in turn came to be the same people who felt that seniority or one's formal title in the corporate hierarchy was no longer the basis for automatic deference. What I saw emerging were new mental postures—entirely new ways of defining meaning, what we valued, and our place and prospects in this world.

In 1989, we all witnessed European communism collapse under the weight of its own hypocrisy because people stopped believing. In a less dramatic but still profound fashion, the old order in Canada collapsed in the latter half of the twentieth century, a process I document in *Sex in the Snow*.

Values once thought to be immutable are now evolving, not just in Canada but around the world. Researchers wish to understand this change because we are naturally curious. Our clients wish to understand social change because they wish to survive in an increasingly competitive international business environment with a growing number of interdependent political institutions and non-governmental organizations (NGOs) that try to govern or influence complex market forces.

Environics began tracking social change in Canada in 1983 with our colleagues at CROP in Montreal and in alliance with Alain de Vulpian and his staff at Cofremca in France. Our work was similar to that of Daniel Yankelovich and his partners in the United States, to the VALS (Values and Lifestyles) system developed by Arnold Mitchell and his team at the Stanford Research Institute, and later to Ron Inglehart, Neil Nevitte, and their academic confreres who inaugurated the World Values Study in 1981.

Each of these systems draws from sociological and psychological theory and has in common the use of standard survey research techniques: one-on-one in-depth interviews, focus groups and, most famously, surveys of representative samples of the population with batteries of questions. The Environics system, described more fully in Appendix A, is perhaps unique in the breadth of values monitored, the number of interviews conducted, and the worldwide scope of our activities.

Sex in the Snow describes social change in Canada from mid-century to the end of the millennium. It chronicles not only the aforementioned evolution from conformity to individual autonomy, but also the evolution from delayed gratification to an immediate demand for pleasure, and from a spiritual orientation defined almost solely by traditional Judeo-Christian belief and practice to one that is more eclectic, discerning, and personal.

As Canadians, my colleagues and I had an inborn curiosity about the United States. As Canadian market researchers, we were forced to understand the United States if we wished our company to meet the increasingly global needs of our clients. At the time I wrote *Sex in the Snow* in 1997, we had already fielded two large social values surveys in the United States—the first in 1992 and the second in 1996. I even wrote a short chapter comparing Canadians and Americans in *Sex in the Snow,* but I was not prepared to hazard a book-length treatise until we had completed the 2000 wave of our research and done a lot more background reading, particularly given that so much of what we were seeing ran counter to popular wisdom. By the year 2000, we had amassed a total of 14,413 interviews conducted among representative samples of Canadians and Americans aged fifteen and over. This book represents a decade of field research and two years of computer analysis, reading, and deliberation among my colleagues, followed by the application of digits to keyboards in the drafting of the text.

I had toyed with the idea of following (humbly) in the footsteps of another foreigner, Alexis de Tocqueville of France, by focusing solely on the United States. But in the end I decided to build on the work we had been doing in Canada since 1983 and undertake a comparative analysis of the two cultures, the United States and Canada. In this sense, I follow more closely in the footsteps of one of America's greatest sociologists, Seymour Martin Lipset, who has devoted a significant portion of his more than half-century career to studying our two countries.

Lipset initially wanted to know why Canada had developed a viable social democratic party—the Co-operative Commonwealth Federation (CCF), later renamed the New Democratic Party (NDP)—and why his native land had not. My interest, on the other hand, is to find out why an initially "conservative" society like Canada has ended up producing an autonomous, inner-directed, flexible, tolerant, socially liberal, and spiritually eclectic people while an initially "liberal" society like the United States has ended up producing a people who are, relatively speaking, materialistic, outer-directed, intolerant, socially conservative, and deferential to traditional institutional authority. Why do these two societies seem to prove the law of unintended consequences?

The Environics surveys of social values include an array of more than 300 questions or statements that have been crafted to measure more than 100 social values (listed below). On average, we use three or four questions or statements to capture various aspects of each value. This ensures the robust measurement of several facets of a phenomenon.

The questions or items are placed in different sections of the survey to reduce the bias of inter-item contamination—that is, to reduce the possibility that the answer to a question will be influenced by the one, two, or three questions asked before it. I append the Glossary of the 101 values tracked in the U.S. social values survey (Appendix B) so that readers might know exactly what we mean by terms like "heterarchy" or "meaningful moments."

One of the values tracked, for example, is *Adaptability to Complexity*. It is defined as "Tendency to adapt easily to the uncertainties of modern life, and not to feel threatened by the changes and complexities of society today. A desire to explore this complexity as a learning experience and a source of opportunity." The value *Adaptability to Complexity* is created by aggregating the responses to the following three statements in our survey, with which respondents are asked to agree or disagree:

"I like trying to take advantage of the unforeseen circumstances and opportunities that present themselves."

"I do not feel uncomfortable living with the uncertainties and the unexpected in life today."

"It is not really a problem for me that life is becoming more and more complex."

In total, we are now tracking over 100 social values in Canada and the United States, everything from *Acceptance of Violence* and *Active Government* to *Work Ethic* and *Xenophobia,* as follows:

Acceptance of Violence
Active Government
Adaptability to Complexity
Adaptive Navigation
Advertising as Stimulus
American Dream
Anomie and Aimlessness
Attraction to Crowds
Aversion to Complexity
Brand Apathy
Buying on Impulse
Celebrating Passages
Civic Apathy
Civic Engagement
Community Involvement
Concern for Appearance
Confidence in Advertising
Confidence in Big Business
Confidence in Small Business
Cultural Assimilation
Culture Sampling
Discerning Hedonism
Discriminating Consumerism
Duty
Ecological Concern
Ecological Fatalism
Effort Toward Health
Emotional Control
Enthusiasm for New Technology
Entrepreneurialism
Equal Relationship with Youth
Ethical Consumerism
Everyday Ethics
Everyday Rage
Faith in Science
Fatalism
Fear of Violence

Financial Security
Flexible Families
Flexible Gender Identity
Gender Parity
Global Consciousness
Heterarchy
Holistic Health
Importance of Aesthetics
Importance of Brand
Importance of Spontaneity
Interest in the Unexplained
Introspection and Empathy
Intuition and Impulse
Joy of Consumption
Just Deserts
Largesse Oblige
Living Virtually
Look Good Feel Good
Meaningful Moments
More Power for Business
More Power for Media
More Power for Politics
Multiculturalism
Mysterious Forces
National Pride
Need for Status Recognition
Networking
Obedience to Authority
Ostentatious Consumption
Parochialism
Patriarchy
Penchant for Risk
Personal Challenge
Personal Control
Personal Creativity
Personal Escape
Personal Expression

Primacy of the Family

Propriety

Protection of Privacy

Pursuit of Intensity

Racial Fusion

Rejection of Authority

Rejection of Order

Religion à la Carte

Religiosity

Saving on Principle

Search for Roots

Selective Use of Personal Services

Sensualism

Sexism

Sexual Permissiveness

Skepticism of Advertising

Social Intimacy

Social Responsibility

Spiritual Quest

Technology Anxiety

Time Stress

Traditional Family

Traditional Gender Identity

Vitality

Voluntary Simplicity

Work Ethic

Xenophobia

As is evident in perusing our list of values, we are not using this term as one would in everyday life, as in "Canadian values," "family values," or "religious values." This colloquial use of the term implies that values means good values or ethics, ones we all admire or should admire. Consequently, we often hear the epithet "He has no values" as a criticism of someone who does not tell the truth or cheats other people. Our use of the term "values" implies no judgment on their goodness, but rather that they are ideas that motivate people to behave the way they do, good, bad, or neither. It is not for us to say that the father of the family should or should not be the master of the house—to take the example of an item we use to measure orientation to patriarchal authority. (A Latin American sociologist, who also happens to be a woman, visiting Toronto for a gathering of academics, recently interrupted my presentation by asking incredulously, "But who else would be?" implying that the father's domestic mastery was as obvious to her as the Earth being round and chiding me for asking such a superfluous, if not stupid, question.) Similarly, we make no judgment about the value *Ostentatious Consumption,* first identified as "conspicuous consumption" by the brilliant American economist Thorstein Veblen in 1899 when America's nouveau riche in the Gilded Age began purchasing the trappings of European aristocracy as symbols of the respectability and prestige to which they aspired. Equally, we do not judge, or at least try not to judge, such values as *Anomie and Aimlessness,*

Everyday Rage, Acceptance of Violence, and *Xenophobia*. They exist in our cultures, and as social scientists we must try as best we can to understand, leaving it to others to lament the decline of traditional virtues.

In this book, as in all my work, my personal goal is to be as detached (sometimes ironically so) as I possibly can from all social segments, including my own, and to retain my sense of humour even in the face of evidence that we humans are as prone to folly as to wisdom.

THIS BOOK IS THE STORY OF SOCIAL CHANGE in North America based on three snapshot surveys in the United States and Canada over the past decade. To provide context to the narrative, I look for historical antecedents and contemporary evidence that the values our survey respondents claim for themselves are actually expressed in behaviour. At the end of the book, I reflect on our research and speculate what it might mean for the wider debate on globalization.

The opening chapter, entitled "Americans Retrench," sketches the basic story of recent social change in the United States and tells the surprising story of regression to a more traditional mindset during a decade of peace and nearly unprecedented prosperity in that country.

The second chapter, "North America's Two Distinct Societies," examines in detail the current state of both the United States and Canada when it comes to values that define meaning, everyday life, consumption, and community—to flesh out the general claim that, culturally, Canadians are not being steadily transformed into Americans in parkas.

The third chapter, "Looking Within: American Diversity, Canadian Consensus," describes the major regional cultures of North America, revisiting, in some way, Joel Garreau's *Nine Nations of North America*. Here I describe the characteristics of the continent's major regions, nine in the United States and seven in Canada. I show that forces such as mobility, education, communications, materialism, multiculturalism, and public policies are reducing the influence of geography on values in Canada, but surprisingly are having much less effect in the United States, where regional differences still remain significant.

Also in this chapter I discuss North American demographic groups, with special attention to youth on both sides of the border, to explore the hypothesis that the effects of the forces of Americanization will be most pronounced among Canada's young people, who, like the canary in the coal mine, should be the first to confirm Canada's inevitable convergence with the values Americans hold dear.

The fourth chapter, "Separated at Birth," explains why the cultures of these two countries are different and suggests a few hypotheses as to why we are seeing a divergence of values at the turn of this millennium. I look at the founding values, experiences, and institutions in each country and how these initial differences express themselves in the way we live today on each side of the border.

The fifth chapter, "Clouds on the Canadian Horizon," sketches the story of social change in Canada and discusses the rather dramatic retrenchment in the mid-1990s—a storm cloud, as the title suggests, in the otherwise tranquil Canadian socio-cultural weather forecast.

Finally, in my concluding chapter, "The Myth of Inevitability," I reflect on the larger theme of this book: the myth, I believe, that Canada is well on its way to absorption into the United States. In it I review the evolution of social change in the two countries and speculate about why, after taking divergent paths in our early histories, our values tended to converge earlier in the twentieth century, but have more recently moved apart. I then go on to discuss what the story of the United States and Canada might mean for other countries in the world and for the wider debate on globalization and cultural convergence. I end, because I am a Canadian genetically inoculated against triumphalism, with the coda that Canada's evolution in a trajectory distinct from that of the United States may be probable, but is not a certainty.

The first appendix that follows sets out in detail the Environics approach to social values research. Subsequent appendices include a glossary of the social values we track, the list of graphic figures in the book, a list of states in each region of the U.S., the American/North American socio-cultural maps referred to in the text, a description of the Canadian socio-cultural map and quadrants referred to in the text, a note to readers who may wish to compare their social values with those of others, and a bibliography of books consulted in the preparation of this work.

This book is primarily intended for a Canadian audience, but I hope it may be of interest to Americans who may be intrigued by a glimpse of a country so seemingly near and yet with mental postures far from their own. Europeans, Australians, and even the Queen's subjects in Tony Blair's Britain who are ambivalent about American influence on their societies might also find some useful lessons in the Canada–U.S. nexus.

I believe that Canadians—immersed in the rhetoric of globalization, surrounded by dizzying economic and technological change, and wondering whether there will still be a place in the world for their unique values and perspective—will be somewhat comforted that at least one Canadian believes that a Canadian way of living and thinking will endure well into the future.

one

AMERICANS RETRENCH

Sometimes I think the thing I'll mind about death is not so
much not being alive but no longer being an American.
—John Updike, *Toward the End of Time*

I know you're all going to think this is crazy,
but I always thought Jesus was an American.
—A University of California student in a seminar
on first-century history, quoted by Mark Slouka

Thus, in the moral world everything is classified, coordinated, foreseen, and
decided in advance. In the world of politics everything is in turmoil, contested,
and uncertain. In the one case obedience is passive, though voluntary; in the other
there is independence, contempt of experience, and jealousy of all authority.
—Alexis de Tocqueville, *Democracy in America*

FRENCH THINKER AND POLITICIAN Alexis de Tocqueville wrote the above-quoted words in 1831, but over 170 years later, they still register the crucial tension of American life: the great national struggle between personal independence and moral order. Tocqueville marvelled at the paucity of the legal constraints to which Americans were prepared to submit. Compared with the Old World and its slow-dying feudalism, America and its liberty-obsessed egalitarianism must have seemed foreign beyond all imagining. Describing the society that English emigrants to the New World had created in New England by the mid-seventeenth century, Tocqueville cooed, "Democracy more perfect than any of which antiquity had dared to dream sprang full-grown and fully armed from the midst of the old feudal society."

But the Frenchman was also amazed at the social constraints that Americans accepted readily: if their laws required little of them, their small, pious communities set standards of conduct more exacting than any legislator would dare impose. Although the whispering threat of small-town gossip helped to keep many early Americans' behaviour in check, above all it was the strict sectarian spirit of the nation that guided citizens' actions and caused Tocqueville to remark that "while the law allows the American people to do everything, there are things which religion prevents them from imagining and forbids them to dare."

If the gush of unabashed sex and violence that has emerged from Hollywood during the past thirty years is any indication of the national climate, then it is probably no longer true that religion prevents Americans from *imagining* much. But there is considerable controversy regarding how many things religion "forbids them to dare." Devoutly religious Americans have been wringing their hands for decades about the diminishing hold of religion in general and Christianity in particular over their society. It's crucial to maintain individual liberty, most would say, but individual liberty sure does work nicely when all those free individuals operate within similarly strict personal moral frameworks, preferably frameworks handed down from a single divine source.

At the same time, non-religious and many moderately religious Americans hear that the membership rolls of evangelical churches and orthodox synagogues are swelling year after year, and see George W. Bush in the Oval Office (he who, as governor of Texas, declared 10 June "Jesus Day"—so much for the separation of Church and the Lone Star State) and do a little hand-wringing of their own. To them, the moral order that social conservatives complain has nearly disappeared seems much less endangered than the rights and freedoms of dissenting individuals and minority groups. Perhaps they forget that the early pilgrims and others escaping persecution in Europe had come to America in search of religious freedom for themselves, not others.

*"Religious freedom is my immediate goal, but my
long-range plan is to go into real estate."*

And, of course, America being America, the rhetoric surrounding social change in the U.S. tends to be writ particularly large. It can seem especially overblown when beheld from the quieter, more moderate place north of the 49th parallel. I sometimes wonder, How can we—who are so staid that we experienced a week-long national frisson at the sight of a wetsuited Stockwell Day arriving at a press conference via jet-ski—even begin to understand the fevered, moralistic social and political discourse that unfolds so close to our border yet so far from our timid, pragmatic, compromise-crafting culture?

The United States is, after all, the country in which Jerry Falwell could assert on national television that the attacks of 11 September were at least in part the fault of a too-secular American society—that the terrorists were actually instruments of a Christian God so enraged by the American Civil Liberties Union that He decided to bring down ruination upon the nation's head. It is also the country in which expatriate British journalist Christopher Hitchens complains vociferously about religion's stranglehold on national media and politics. Hitchens is so determined in his quest to unravel what he would call America's uncritical reverence for all things religious (or at least all things purportedly Christian) that he has written a book debunking the idea of Mother Teresa's saintliness. Neither Falwell nor Hitchens is representative of Americans at large, but they are two of the extreme voices in national debates—and it is utterly impossible to imagine either of them in the Canadian political landscape. Who might our Hitchens be? Maude Barlow? Naomi Klein? Our Falwell: Preston Manning? *One Hundred Huntley Street*'s somewhat less than charismatic host David Mainse? One might have any of these Canadians over to dinner (or all of them—on the same night!), and the odds would be fairly good that the word "evil" would not be hurled even once.

It is little wonder, then, that we Canadians sometimes find our neighbours baffling. Between their rhetoric and our own (the left's admonitions about the dangers of convergence with the gun-toting free marketeers to the south, the right's insistence that we shed our outdated national differences like garments on a long-awaited wedding night and join our industrious, innovative Yankee friends in an orgy of free trade and economic growth), Americans are reflected in so many funhouse mirrors that it would be remarkable if we saw them, collectively, as anything other than caricatures. I have long dreamt, therefore, of offering my fellow Canadians a look at our neighbours to the south through a lens quite different from any offered by advertisers or political partisans. The lens I offer here is the most telling and robust one I have come across in my more than thirty years as a social researcher: the lens of social values measurement.

What has been the nature of social change in America, particularly during the last decade? Is America, as many contend, in the final days of a long, steady moral decline? Are Americans becoming, like Canadians and Europeans, increasingly "postmodern," leaving behind religious and other kinds of authority in favour of enlightened personal autonomy? Is

American society divided into two groups of "culture warriors," one group urban, secular, and located along both coasts, the other rural, religious, and deeply rooted in the "heartland"? And above all, where is Pierre Trudeau's self-centred American elephant headed?

The Environics social values system helps answer these questions. The polling data we have amassed over the past decade, which were briefly described in the Introduction, have allowed us to create a map that shows the trajectory of social change in America. That is, by tracking thousands of Americans' responses to hundreds of questions over time, we have been able to graphically represent the changing position of U.S. society on a social values map and gain a sense of what America's overall mental posture has been, and how it is changing. This method also allows us to plot various segments of the U.S. population in order to demonstrate visually those whose social values are similar (for example, Americans who live along the Pacific coast tend to fall very near New Englanders on our socio-cultural map) and those whose social values are vastly disparate (it should come as no surprise that when we plot respondents who identify themselves as fundamentalist Christians, they show up on the opposite end of the map from those who identify themselves as atheists or agnostics).

Social values maps tend to differ in appearance from one society to another. This is because the key axes of social values that define one society may be relatively insignificant in another country. In the Introduction, I described the manner in which we create "values" by grouping together questions that seek to measure a single aspect of an individual's mental posture (the example I used was *Adaptability to Complexity*). Once we have gathered data on our respondents' adherence to (or abhorrence of) these values, multivariate computer analysis identifies the main dimensions of social change in the society we are examining, and then plots those dimensions onto a two-dimensional graphic space: what we call a socio-cultural map. In the United States, the two axes that are the most significant indicators of social change, and thus most useful in a graphic representation of the population's social values, are "Authority versus Individuality" and "Survival versus Fulfillment."

The Authority–Individuality axis is the vertical axis; the values associated with deference to authority are located largely at the top of the map, while those associated with individuality are at the bottom. Although our map axes require simple titles such as those we have assigned them, both axes are rich spectrums that illuminate a great deal of information. Our vertical axis, for example, is not simply about authority and individuality in the collo-quial sense of each term. The north end of the axis has a great deal to do with conformity to the expectations of authority figures, but also registers a willingness to obey the customs and demands of institutions and ideologies. Those Americans at the top of our socio-cultural map are more likely to believe in obedience to the dictates of religious leaders, more likely to believe that "the father of the family must be master in his own house," and more likely to believe that in the world of business things work best when there's one clear leader who tells others what to do. Therefore, it is in the top quarter of the map that we find trends like *Obedience to Authority*, belief in *Traditional Family*, *Religiosity*, and *Patriarchy*.

The United States Socio-Cultural Map:
North–South Axis and Selected Trends

It's not just that the people whose values place them close to the top of our map need or wish to be told what to do by someone specific—a priest, a father, a boss. They also tend to believe that there is one right way to do most things, even if no one in particular has articulated it. Therefore, at the top of the map we find trends like *Propriety, Everyday Ethics, Duty,* and *Work Ethic.* Even if no one has told these people that they need to show up for work at 9:00 a.m. sharp, tie neatly tied, they will because they sense an implicit imperative to do so, and they believe that obeying such imperatives is the right and proper way to live. These people likely suppressed squeals of glee (of course, it would be impolite to let out an actual squeal) upon hearing that George W. Bush had reinstituted a suit-and-tie dress code at the White House. At last, they sighed, some decorum in the highest office in the land.

At the bottom of the map, the "Individuality" end of the spectrum, we find those who are comparatively unwilling to defer to authority. These Americans say, Leave the "Yes, Sir, no, Sir" rules where they belong: in the 1950s. Those whose values place them at the bottom of the map are interested in making their own choices about all aspects of life: they want the freedom to decide what kind of family to have (and yes, these Americans insist, there *are* different kinds of families), what kind of God (if any) to believe in, and, on a more mundane level, what to wear to work. These people are likely to sport that now-venerable "Question Authority" bumper sticker on their cars, but they're willing to do more than question: if they feel strongly enough, they will reject authority altogether—leaving the church, for example, or saying goodbye to their bosses and starting their own businesses, or escaping loser males for an unforgettable road trip à la *Thelma and Louise,* or taking on the system in *Erin Brockovich* style.

Thus, on the lower half of the map we find those who believe that young people need not necessarily defer to their elders in all matters (this trend is labelled *Equal Relationship with Youth),* who believe in the *Rejection of Authority,* and who are open to *Flexible Families* and *Flexible Gender Identities.* People toward the bottom of the map also tend to believe that work gets done most effectively not when people are organized into a strict, unchanging hierarchy, but when leadership is fluid—when whoever is best suited to take charge of a given project (whoever has the time, the interest, and the skills—not just the person with the highest title) can step into a position of leadership (we call this trend *Heterarchy*).

It's easy to assign simplistic stereotypes to the extremes of the map: the retired Colonel at the top whose wife gets an earful if dinner isn't hot when it reaches the table; the self-absorbed, narcissistic Baby Boomer who finds any kind of sacrifice or commitment intolerable. But these caricatures are not entirely accurate or fair. The Authority versus Individuality axis displays a range of interrelated and deeply embedded values.

In essence, those at the top of the map are more devoted to order of all kinds; they appreciate predictability, stability, and ritual. They believe in national order (immigrants should assimilate and leave their old ways behind), familial order (a family is a married man and woman with kids—and Dad's the boss and principal breadwinner), sexual order (people should adhere to traditional gender roles—no experimentation in dress, behaviour, or relationships), and social order (propriety, courtesy, etiquette).

Those at the bottom of the map are more flexible—more open to change, informality, and experimentation, including an à la carte approach to life: a little of this religion, family structure, gender trait, lifestyle, and a little of that. Some are very deliberate about their rejection of old rules and institutions. These people might, for example, refuse to marry on principle, rejecting the formal sanction of Church and State, even though they hope to be in a lifelong monogamous relationship and produce and raise offspring. Others are simply doing what they see as practical: maybe they wish they could have avoided a divorce, or wish their kids had waited a little longer before becoming sexually active, but they're not about to defer to what they consider to be anachronistic social conventions just because some book or preacher says they should. Guilt for these people is something that should arise from within, from one's own sense of right and wrong, not be laid on by some external authority.

The U.S. social values map becomes significantly richer and more nuanced as we introduce the second axis: the horizontal Survival versus Fulfillment axis. On the left-hand side of the axis—the Survival end—we find, as the axis label suggests, values associated with raw survival and material gain. (At Environics we sometimes call this the "axis of evil.") At the leftmost end of the map there is no idealism; here are the values of brutal competition and zero-sum social interaction: kill or be killed. Americans at the most extreme end of this axis think people get their *Just Deserts*, and they are determined to "get theirs." If obtaining what they want and feel they deserve means they have to exclude people *(Sexism, Xenophobia)*, use their fists *(Acceptance of Violence)*, or do some damage to Mother Nature *(Ecological Fatalism)*, then so be it.

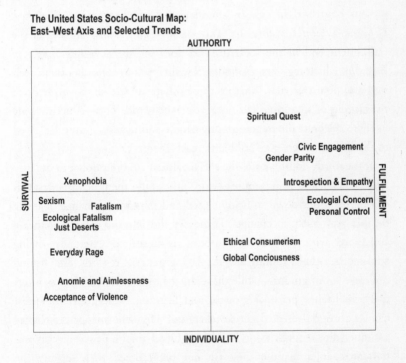

The United States Socio-Cultural Map: East–West Axis and Selected Trends

Also falling at the leftmost end of the Survival–Fulfillment continuum are values that demonstrate the stress of seeing the world through Darwin-tinted glasses. People who fall at the extreme left of the map are more likely to report feeling *Everyday Rage* and a sense of generalized hostility to and alienation from the world around them *(Anomie and Aimlessness)*.

At the other end of this spectrum, on the Fulfillment side, we find those values that are more concerned with quality of life than with standard of living. Americans who fall at this end of the horizontal axis are likely to have a more "postmaterialist" outlook on life. They don't feel threatened by the world around them (whether because of material circumstances, personal character, or mental posture), and they don't feel compelled to struggle ruthlessly for success. They are less interested in getting ahead and more interested in personal growth and well-being, as well as in improving society at large.

The idealistic values that are lacking on the left side of the map are present on the right side in abundance: *Civic Engagement, Ecological Concern, Ethical Consumerism,* and *Global Consciousness* all fall on the Fulfillment end of the spectrum. So does the trend *Introspection and Empathy,* which registers respondents' willingness to consider others' feelings and points of view, whether those others are friends, co-workers, or the citizens of a country halfway around the world. These Americans are likely to celebrate differences among people and regions, and to feel open to the lessons others may be able to teach them.

If the north–south axis of the social values map boils down to order—who wants it, and who is more at ease without it—then the east–west axis of the map boils down to being closed and resistant to change or being flexible and open to change. Those on the left side of the map are concerned with survival and success as measured externally—being admired by others, gaining and displaying material rewards, establishing exclusive social groups—while those on the right side seek success internally: in health, personal growth, and learning. Americans who resist change are outer-directed status seekers and those who are open to change are inner-directed, achieving fulfillment by relying on personal goals and standards. It is because they are not preoccupied with seeking the approval of the herd that the inner-directed in America are not closed and hostile to complexity, but rather open and empathetic.

I hope the reader will forgive me for this rather counterintuitive description of the values on the "left" of our socio-cultural map, since most people on the left of the political spectrum would abhor many of these values. Lefties, however, can take comfort in the fact that, on our map at least, the values they admire are right.

Havina described the two axes, we can now look at the map's four quadrants before moving on to see where Americans lie in this "social values space" and how they are moving around it over time. An examination of the individual quadrants proves highly instructive as we seek to understand social change in the United States: each quadrant is a psychographic landscape in which a complex but coherent worldview can be found.

The United States Socio-Cultural Map:
Mental Postures of the Quadrants

AUTHORITY

Status & Security:
Obedience to Traditional Structures and Norms

Authenticity & Responsibility:
Well-Being, Harmony, and Responsibility

SURVIVAL

FULFILLMENT

Exclusion & Intensity:
Seeking Stimulus and Attention

Idealism & Autonomy:
Exploration and Flexibility

INDIVIDUALITY

The following profiles are, of necessity, stereotypes. Not many Americans would buy the entire values profile of their quadrant. Individuals' worldviews are more nuanced than any analysis of this kind can comprehend. That said, it is worth noting that this map has been constructed by the attitudes it measures—not the other way around. Because the map's layout is determined by correlations among individual trends, the patterns of values in these quadrants have emerged quite organically from Americans' responses to survey questions. The world-views contained within each of these quadrants emerge on our map precisely because they tend to hang together in the minds of Americans (albeit often unconsciously). Respondents are not just being plotted onto a template dreamed up by an expert with a computer—survey responses actually create the mapspace in which they are analyzed. (More information on the map and how it is constructed can be found in the Introduction and in Appendix A.)

Moving clockwise from the upper left of the map:

We have labelled the upper left area of the map the **Status and Security** quadrant.[1] This quadrant combines the deferential tendencies of the upper half of the map with the outward-directed, survivalist tendencies of the left-hand side.

Americans whose values would locate them in this quarter of the map believe in pursuing the American Dream by following the rules. They have a strong desire to achieve material success, and to display the symbols of that success to others (in this quadrant, those symbols are likely to be relatively traditional ones like Cadillacs, big houses, and Rolex watches). If they have not already done so, these Americans are planning to achieve affluence and security through personal industry and discipline; they would never consider lying, cheating, or stealing their way to the top, as might their less scrupulous compatriots farther down the map. They play by the rules, whether in the game of life or in the game of golf, which for many retirees in this quadrant is the same thing.

Because striving for social approval is such a priority for these Americans, they seek well-defined norms and standards of behaviour. If they're going to win at the game of American life, those in this quadrant reason, they need to know exactly what the rules are. The rules these

---

1. Readers wishing to see the positioning of the values in this and the other three quadrants are invited to visit Appendix E, figures E1 to E4.

people have absorbed (and will likely never abandon) are not only economic (work hard, dress for success, "save your pennies, and the dollars will take care of themselves"), but also social. For this quadrant, men should be men, women women. Dad brings home the bacon, and he's king of his own domestic castle. You go to church on Sunday, and you respect your president (unless he happens to be that philanderer Clinton). And if you don't like the rules, you're welcome to move to Sweden. (Or Canada.)

In its most troubling form, these Americans' desire to belong to and elicit the approval of a cohesive social group can lead to a certain hostility toward out-groups. Hence this quadrant's *Xenophobia*. Those in the upper-left quadrant sense that their world is changing, and view almost all of that change as deterioration. Some changes are merely unnerving to these Americans (the value *Technology Anxiety*, for example, resides in this quadrant), but they view many, such as the changing form of the family, high levels of immigration, and the advances of feminism, as not only worrisome but verging on the immoral.

To the right of the Status and Security quadrant, we find the mental posture labelled **Authenticity and Responsibility** (Appendix E, Figure E2). On the vertical axis, these Americans are level with the Status and Security quadrant: the two groups are equally deferential to authority and inclined toward order. Falling closer to the Fulfillment end of the horizontal axis, however, those in the Authenticity and Responsibility quadrant are less preoccupied with outward displays of success and social standing, and are more concerned with enhancing the quality of their lives as measured from within.

The deference to authority in the Authenticity and Responsibility quadrant is of a more religious nature than in the Status and Security quadrant. Those in the upper-right portion of the map register a high degree of religiosity, which informs their strong belief in the importance of the *Traditional Family*. The trend *Spiritual Quest* also resides in this quadrant, indicating that these Americans take great interest in their personal spiritual growth. They are not only interested in the moral edicts of their faith, but also see religiosity as an important means of long-term personal development.

There is stronger nationalism in the upper-right quadrant than in the upper left. Those in the Authenticity and Responsibility quarter believe in the *American Dream,* register great *National Pride,* and believe that immigrants who come to America should leave their old cultures and identities behind and become "unhyphenated Americans" (this is the value we've labelled *Cultural Assimilation*). These Americans reason that if their own ancestors shed their past when they came to America, some willing and others eager to adopt new anglicized names, why shouldn't all subsequent waves of immigrants do the same? The ideology of multiculturalism, they would argue, serves only to hold immigrants back from truly enjoying the promise of the American Dream they have realized. *E pluribus unum.*

The nationalist values of the Authenticity and Responsibility quadrant are, however, far from the *Xenophobia* of the upper-left quadrant on our map. Here we find a nationalism that is simply a large-scale version of the civic engagement that pervades this upper-right quadrant. Those in the Authenticity and Responsibility quadrant, with their emphasis on *Social Intimacy, Social Responsibility,* and *Everyday Ethics,* seek personal fulfillment in their social relationships—even in the relatively loose bonds they may share with neighbours or fellow members of local clubs or service organizations. And just as those in the upper-right quadrant take pride in their community attachments, they also take pride in America and think others should too. It is in this quadrant that we find many of those fabled soccer moms, not to mention the generous dads who coach Little League baseball and drive Junior's friends home in the minivan. These are the swing voters who elect American presidents.

The social responsibility and modest progressiveness that characterize this quadrant suggest that the value of *Cultural Assimilation* in this context is not so much racist or xenophobic as traditionally patriotic. In part, it is probably a symptom of this quadrant's *Aversion to Complexity;* for in a society where complexity abounds, these people regret, even disapprove, when immigrants retain the languages, customs, and spiritual practices of their home countries.

Denizens of the Authenticity and Responsibility quadrant pay considerable attention to their own personal well-being. In addition to their commitment to religious practice, they are likely to make an effort to live a healthful lifestyle and to approach their personal well-being from a holistic perspective. For many, mealtime still means sitting down around the table as a family, saying grace, and enjoying one of Mom's specialties. The health- and wellness-oriented trends in this quadrant are outgrowths of this side of the map's penchant for personal fulfillment.

Moving down the map from the Authenticity and Responsibility quadrant, we find the most postmodern region of the American map: the **Idealism and Autonomy** quadrant (Appendix E, Figure E3). This quadrant is much less deferential to traditional forms of authority than is the Authenticity and Responsibility quadrant, but shares the latter's drive toward fulfillment. Thus, we find those in the Idealism and Autonomy quadrant seeking personal fulfillment not through traditional institutional channels such as the Church, and not necessarily through the traditional family, but through avenues they craft themselves: social, familial, spiritual, and professional.

The Americans who are likely to fall into this quadrant are, as the quadrant title suggests, extremely autonomous. They are unlikely to submit to the dictates of religious leaders, political elites, or the family patriarch. They find making their own (sometimes unique) life decisions enriching, and because they see matters of family structure, sexuality, and spirituality as deeply personal, they are likely to bristle at the idea of anyone—whether Pat Robertson, George Bush, or Martha Stewart—telling them what to do.

It would be wrong to assume that all the individualism and fulfillment-seeking we find in this quadrant implies that this portion of the map is the domain of the self-obsessed. The values of this region of the map indicate that the penchant for personal fulfillment here does not rest upon a world-view that is closed to the world. Indeed, containing the trends *Global Consciousness, Ecological Concern,* and *Culture Sampling,* this quadrant boasts the most broad-minded, least self-centred values in America. These are individualists who have a healthy tolerance for the individualism of others.

We find a great deal of flexibility and openness to change in this quadrant, and these values are clearly consistent with the lower right's interest in autonomy and personal control. Naturally, if one wants the freedom to adopt a lifestyle and philosophy of one's own choosing, it is only reasonable to embrace the principle that everyone should be accorded the same freedom. The Idealism and Autonomy quadrant's interest in flexibility is also bound up in its idealism. Having rejected the old rules (and rulers) embraced by those farther up the map, Americans in this quadrant have their eyes and ears open to new sources of meaning and concepts of social organization that they hope will prove more egalitarian, inclusive, and ecologically sound than the traditional models.

Paul Ray's socially liberal and ecologically concerned "Cultural Creatives" are floating around in this quadrant, as are David Brooks's "Bobos" (Bourgeois Bohemians, whom Brooks describes as embracing the countercultural bohemianism of the Beat generation and 1960s hippies while also displaying the industriousness and market-savvy of the American bourgeois middle class once personified by Benjamin Franklin). Bobo-watchers will be interested to note that we find the trend of *Entrepreneurialism* in this quadrant alongside all the idealism and autonomy trends.

Moving left now to examine our final quadrant, the lower-left **Exclusion and Intensity** segment (Appendix E, Figure E4), we find a set of values informed by a rejection of authority, and also by an outer-directed emphasis on survival and materialism.

In this quadrant, we find not one but *two* distinct mental postures. On the centre right-hand side of this lower-left region of the map, we find a number of hedonistic, pleasure- and thrill-seeking values: *Sexual Permissiveness, Penchant for Risk, Buying on Impulse, Pursuit of Intensity, Importance of Aesthetics*. Americans in this region of the map are likely to be open to risks of all kinds—whether they be participation in extreme sports that inspire the head-shaking awe of others, or financial risks (legal or otherwise) that will hopefully pay off and yield some flashy new "toys." In either case, it is not just the results (namely the hoped-for admiration of others) but the adrenaline-producing process of taking the risk that appeal to these (predominantly young, male) Americans.

It is noteworthy that the risk-taking impulse in this area of the map correlates with the outer-directed consumption trends such as *Ostentatious Consumption, Importance of Aesthetics,* and *Buying on Impulse.* Denizens of this region of the map are more likely than other Americans to seek attention and recognition in any way they can—be it through risky behaviour or showy clothes, cars, and gadgets. Above all, they want to stand out; for every step the quadrant above them (Status and Security) takes to be admired by fitting in, those on the right side of this lower-left quadrant take a step in the opposite direction, trying to be admired for standing apart from the crowd.

The left side of this quadrant has a harder edge, and news of its growth during the past decade will likely be unsettling to many. This left-hand side of the Exclusion and Intensity quadrant is disturbing because it is the most nihilistic space in our social values map. Like the Idealism and Autonomy quadrant, this quadrant finds traditional forms of authority (religious, political, patriarchal) uncompelling. (The only way many of these people will achieve the American Dream is to win it in Las Vegas or steal it.) But unlike the idealists in the lower-right quarter of the map, the denizens of this part of the Exclusion and Intensity quadrant have not replaced the old edicts with new, personal sources of meaning and direction. They have neither the fulfillment-oriented ideals of the quadrant to their right, nor the rigid adherence to traditional rules we find in the Status and Security quadrant directly above them. And as their detached, often hostile values show us, when your rulebook contains neither your own rules nor anyone else's, very little is left in the way of spiritual, social, or ethical direction. Their law is the law of the jungle.

People in this quadrant are the most socially disconnected of any on our map. The trends of *Civic Apathy* and *Anomie and Aimlessness* both reside here, as do *Everyday Rage* and *Acceptance of Violence,* which indicate some of the stress and generalized hostility that emerge from this quadrant's alienation and which can be found among alienated white suburban youth, desperate African-American youth in the ghetto, and younger members of crackpot rural militias.

If the young people in the lower-*right* quadrant were the ones who went to the anti-globalization demonstrations in Seattle and Washington with a dream of sending a message and changing the world, the young people in the lower-left quadrant were more likely to have shown up just to witness and revel in the general chaos—and possibly engage in some serendipitous looting. Rockstar Games may have had a portion of this lower-left quadrant in mind when they created the video game State of Emergency, an "urban-riot game" that simulates the chaotic environment of a mass demonstration against a fictional trade summit. The game's promotional material invites players to "Complete missions in Progressive mode, or just roam the streets causing mayhem in Freeplay mode."

In 2002, the virtual landscape of American teens in this quadrant was augmented by the popular PlayStation 2 game Grand Theft Auto: Vice City, a criminally stylish driving and shooting simulation game in which players are invited to pose as a vicious criminal named Tommy Vercetti, who in order to get out of "glamorous, hedonistic" Vice City, must battle biker gangs, Cuban gangsters, and corrupt politicians. Tommy earns money for his sinister acts, which include running over pedestrians, hiring and then murdering prostitutes, and killing other gangsters with guns, Uzis, swords, and Molotov cocktails. Theoretically, this R-rated game, sold at Toys "R" Us and rated number one on *Entertainment Weekly*'s ten-best-games list for 2002, is targeted at older teens, but it quickly became a hot item for the pre-teen market. A stocking-stuffer that pleased many a little darling on Christmas Day.

Young Americans also flocked to the movie *8 Mile*. In this 2002 hit, white rapper Eminem takes over where Marlon Brando *(The Wild One)*, James Dean *(Rebel Without a Cause)*, Elvis Presley (every one of his movies), and John Travolta *(Saturday Night Fever)* left off. Like his iconic forebears, Eminem is the outsider, the alienated youth both incapable of and unwilling to be socialized into mainstream American life. But it is not just his testosterone-laced volatility that sets him apart from his peers and elders; it is also his talent.

Interesting racial currents run through the movie. Eminem, like Elvis Presley and others before him, participates in (or, depending on whom you ask, appropriates) a predominantly black pop music tradition. He even achieves ascendancy in a primarily black social and artistic scene by being passionately self-assured, and by being better than his black rival Clarence at "keeping shit real" (Clarence has sold out by going to a private school).

In his triumphal final scene, our boy (having rejected mainstream social and economic striving/participation) walks alone down a dark alley, deeper into the lower-left quadrant, with his back to the world: the heroic warrior entirely on his own in a Darwinist dystopia, leaving us with the message that you can't trust anyone but yourself. Take that, Alexis de Tocqueville.

Having now illuminated the mental postures that inform the various regions of the social values map, we have a sense of the psychographic space in which U.S. social change is unfolding. As ought to be clear by now, the socio-cultural map is not a mere backdrop to social change in America. The map is, rather, constituted of the social values Americans hold, and in order to understand the state of the Union and the nature of social change in America, we now need only see what proportions of the U.S. population reside in which areas of the map, and where, on the whole, the population is migrating within the mapspace.

Ron Inglehart's World Values Survey team, including University of Toronto's Neil Nevitte, concluded that societies generally exhibit similar kinds of socio-cultural change as they proceed along the path of industrialization and post-industrialization. People in pre-industrial societies hold traditional values, which include extreme deference to authority, especially religious authority, and a general wariness of change, including an aversion to social mobility. Industrial societies manifest more modern values, replacing deference to religious authority with adherence to rational-legal authority and demonstrating increased achievement motivation and a strong commitment to economic growth. Modernity values money and all the things (material status symbols) that money can buy. Post-industrial societies exhibit postmodern values, which implies that people in them are more autonomous and less deferential to all kinds of authority and that their commitment to rapid economic growth (as they become increasingly able to take basic survival for granted) is supplanted by subjective human concerns relating to quality of life. Postmodern values also include flexibility and an increasing tolerance for diversity of all kinds.

During the description of the various quadrants of our socio-cultural map, it became clear that the lower-right quadrant was by far the most postmodern region of the U.S. map. Its focus on autonomy, its flexibility, its openness to change and diversity, and its emphasis on quality of life over material concerns all indicate that the Idealism and Autonomy quadrant is the stomping ground of America's postmoderns.

Therefore, if America's development were proceeding in the manner of other advanced industrial nations, we would see more and more Americans' values placing them in this lower-right quadrant. But America is not like other advanced industrial nations. "American exceptionalism," as this Yankee uniqueness is known, is certainly apparent when it comes to social change. Americans are not, like Canadians and Western Europeans, proceeding down the map away from religious, patriarchal, and traditional political authority, while also edging to the right of the map in a quest for fulfillment through autonomy and new modes of social engagement. Instead, the U.S. population at large is sliding down and *left* into the Exclusion and Intensity quadrant.

In 1992, our survey of a representative sample of Americans over the age of fifteen placed the population, on the whole, in the Authenticity and Responsibility quadrant, just barely above the halfway mark on the vertical axis (that is, just barely on the Authority half of the map) and slightly to the right of the middle point (or, slightly more oriented toward fulfillment than survival). In 1996, Americans' overall values placed them quite squarely in the centre of the map—they had drifted down and to the left. Looking at the data in 1996, one might have been forgiven for predicting (or hoping) that the population might do an about-face, proceeding right along the map in the coming years to follow the postmodern path of Idealism and Autonomy that other advanced industrial nations have generally travelled. But the 2000 results confirmed the surprising trend that was suggested in 1996: American society was, by and large, headed away from its traditional worldview informed by religiosity and communal responsibility and was drifting into the relatively hostile and nihilistic territory at the bottom left of the map. To the chagrin, I am sure, of both conservative moralists and liberal progressives, social change in America seems to be articulating a rejection of Puritanism and post-modernism alike.

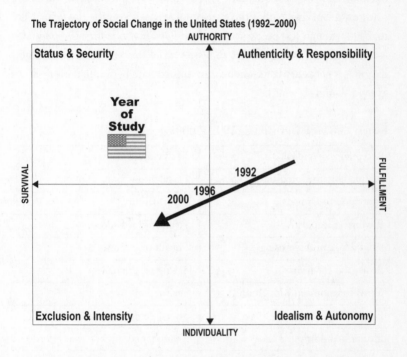

The Trajectory of Social Change in the United States (1992–2000)

I would be the last to assert that the American population—or any population—is uniform. Much of my interest in social values research is rooted in segmentation: the division of societies into groups based on those groups' shared social values. That said, as a sociologist I am in a long-term, sometimes stormy, often rewarding relationship with general-ization. The first step here is to look at the evolution of social values in the U.S. population at large.

When we say Americans are moving down and to the left of the map, we mean they are increasingly embracing the values that reside in the lower-left region of the map. From 1992 to 2000, the trends that rose most markedly were located largely in the Exclusion and Intensity quadrant: these trends included *Acceptance of Violence, Sexism, Penchant for Risk,* and *Ostentatious Consumption. Xenophobia* was among the fastest growing trends (these results are pre-9/11), and although it falls slightly outside the lower-left quadrant it is certainly symptomatic of the move toward the Survival end of the horizontal axis. Also on the rise from 1992 to 2000, though less precipitously, were *Pursuit of Intensity, Confidence in Advertising,* and *Ecological Fatalism* (the belief that environmental degradation is a necessary consequence, an unfortunate byproduct, of life as we know it—and so what).

Fastest Growing U.S. Trends 1992–2000

Acceptance of Violence	Multiculturalism
Adaptability to Complexity	Ostentatious Consumption
Attraction to Crowds	Parochialism
Buying on Impulse	Penchant for Risk
Confidence in Advertising	Pursuit of Intensity
Ecological Fatalism	Saving on Principle
Equal Relationship with Youth	Sexism
Flexible Families	Sexual Permissiveness
Intuition and Impulse	Xenophobia

The values that were declining during this same period are generally in the upper-right Authenticity and Responsibility quadrant. Some of these values are of the very traditional kind and are in long-term decline: *Duty* and *Traditional Family,* for example. Other declining values, though, are more modern and even idealistic: *Introspection and Empathy* (the willingness to put oneself in another's shoes and consider another perspective), *Voluntary Simplicity* (an interest in slowing down one's life and reducing one's consumption), *Ecological Concern, Global Consciousness,* and *Social Intimacy.*

Fastest Declining U.S. Trends 1992–2000

Aversion to Complexity	National Pride
Concern for Appearance	Personal Challenge
Cultural Assimilation	Personal Expression
Discriminating Consumerism	Primacy of the Family
Duty	Rejection of Order
Ecological Concern	Religiosity
Effort Toward Health	Sensualism
Fear of Violence	Spiritual Quest
Global Consciousness	Social Intimacy
Interest in the Unexplained	Time Stress
Introspection and Empathy	Traditional Family
Mysterious Forces	Voluntary Simplicity

What this pattern of social change suggests is that many Americans are shutting themselves off from the world around them, becoming increasingly resigned to living in a competitive jungle where ostentatious consumption and personal thrills rule, and where there is little concern either for the natural environment or for those whose American Dreams have turned into nightmares. *Ecological Fatalism, Ostentatious Consumption,* and *Acceptance of Violence* up, *Introspection and Empathy, Social Intimacy,* and *Global Consciousness* down. At the risk of waxing dystopian, one can almost hear those SUVs rolling into their gated communities, where millions of cable- or satellite-equipped TVs in millions of well-appointed living rooms unobtrusively mutter news about melting polar ice caps, faraway wars, terrorist threats, and the raging violence of American inner cities. Raise the drawbridge, kids, your father's home.

Where does this social drift of American society in general leave us with respect to the question of a so-called "culture war" in America? Does the nation's movement into the lower-left quadrant of the social values map affirm Jerry Falwell's and William Bennett's claims about the moral decay of American society?

Falwell et al. needn't worry about the death of God in the U.S.A. As the likes of Gertrude Himmelfarb and David Frum (a Canadian who left our "socialist gulag" to make good among the harder-edged conservatives south of the border, co-authoring as a White House speechwriter that now-notorious zinger "axis of evil"—from which, perhaps thanks to Mr. Frum, Canada was omitted) are pleased to point out, religious fervour south of the border is on the rise. In her *One Nation, Two Cultures,* Himmelfarb calls the current religious revival the "Fourth Great Awakening" and notes that much of the increase in religiosity in the United States is of the fundamentalist variety.[2]

Its tenacious religiosity is perhaps the characteristic that best distinguishes America from other advanced industrial societies in terms of social change. Seymour Martin Lipset is likely the greatest sociological student of "American exceptionalism" in our era; in his book by that name he writes, "The United States contradicts a statistically-based generalization 'that economic development goes hand in hand with a decline in religious sentiment,' or the agreement among sociologists and Marxists that religion declines as a society modernizes" (p. 62).

Lipset suggests that America's persistent religiosity may be, paradoxically, a result of its strictly enforced separation of Church and State. Whereas in Canada and Europe the church has been linked with the state (and, thus, over time has become subject to the distrust and questioning to which the state has been exposed), in America religion has long been decentralized and congregationally based. The diverse and populist system of American sectarianism has proven much more resilient, in the

---

2. Himmelfarb admits that estimates of fundamentalists' numbers vary broadly, but writes: "The movement as a whole—about 60 million people in 1988, the historian Robert Fogel estimates, or about a fifth of the adult population—is dominated by the fundamentalist, pentecostal, and charismatic Protestant denominations (generally lumped together under the label 'evangelical'); but it also includes as many as 20 million members of the mainline Protestant churches, 6 million 'born again' Catholics, and almost 5 million Mormons" (p. 91).

long run, than the more hierarchical, institutional, state-sanctioned church models of the Old World. Sociologist Rodney Stark has applied economic thinking to the religious "market" in the U.S. Toby Lester paraphrases him thus: "In a free-market religious economy there is a healthy abundance of choice (religious pluralism), which leads naturally to vigorous competition and efficient supply (new and old religious movements). The more competition there is, the higher the level of consumption. This would explain the often remarked paradox that the United States is one of the most religious countries in the world but also one of the strongest enforcers of a separation between Church and State."

The claim that Americans' high levels of religious affiliation can be attributed to U.S. churches, particularly Protestant sects, having been forced to market themselves effectively over the years in order to survive may well be true. According to our data, however, it is not the sects' non-hierarchical organizational structures that are drawing Americans into the fold. We find an extremely strong correlation between deference to authority and religiosity among Americans. Looking back at our socio-cultural map, we find the trend *Religiosity* right next to *Obedience to Authority* at the very top of the Authority axis. Those Americans who describe themselves as "very religious" are far more likely to embrace trends associated with deference to authority—not only *Obedience to Authority* but also *Patriarchy, Traditional Family, Duty,* and *Propriety.* These people are looking for definitive answers and rules to live by, unlike many of those strong on the trend *Spiritual Quest,* who are looking to ask the right questions and wish to arrive at their own, albeit often tentative, conclusions.

Religion is fulfilling a role for Americans that secular institutions do in other countries: safe haven, community, a place to be with "people like me," a refuge from Darwinian competition and conflict in an increasingly dangerous world. Churches are one of the few places, if not the only one, where many Americans feel truly safe—where guns are left at home or under the seat in the 4X4 or checked at the door.

It is perhaps not surprising, given this correlation between religiosity and deference to authority in general, that religiosity is not the only aspect of a more traditional set of social values that remains prominent in the

United States. One of the most striking items we have been tracking during the past decade addresses Americans' orientation to traditional patriarchal authority. In 1992, 1996, and 2000, we asked Americans to strongly agree, agree somewhat, disagree somewhat, or strongly disagree with the statement, "The father of the family must be master in his own house." The aphorism itself comes to us from folklore like "A penny saved is a penny earned" and "Spare the rod and spoil the child." But when social values change so too do our opinions of the wisdom of traditional maxims, sometimes in unexpected ways.

In 1992, 42 per cent of Americans agreed (either strongly or some-what) with that statement. That number seemed high at the time (1992 wasn't so very long ago), but we hadn't, as they say, seen nothing yet. Support for the Father-knows-best credo was actually *on the rise*. In 1996, 44 per cent of respondents agreed with the statement, and in 2000 a full 49 per cent of our sample—almost half the population—agreed that Dad should be boss; this in spite of the frontal assault on patriarchal authority waged by Homer Simpson and Bill Clinton during the 1990s.

This growing acceptance of traditional patriarchal authority is truly remarkable—and seriously divergent with the patterns in other advanced industrial nations. But it is not only *patriarchal* authority that is enjoying increased acceptance among many Americans. When we asked Americans in 1996 whether it was better for one leader to make decisions in a group or whether leadership should be more fluid, 31 per cent agreed with the more hierarchical position that a single leader should call the shots. In 2000, the proportion agreeing with the hierarchical model had shot up seven points to 38 per cent. These Americans were becoming more and more willing to fall in line and do what the boss tells them to do, and this before their president and commander-in-chief began to rally them for a post-9/11 war on terrorism.

Thus far, we've seen that on the whole, American society is drifting toward the lower-left quadrant of our social values map—a region that is willing to suffer very little in the way of authority or rules of any kind. At the same time, as I have just sketched, we find surprising growth in some top-of-the-map trends that are linked to values of the most traditional kind (religiosity, deference to patriarchal authority, belief in hierarchical organizational models). Is this apparent contradiction evidence of the widely discussed "culture war" south of the border, the schism between "red" and "blue" America (red states having voted for Bush and blue ones having voted for Gore), the divide between the liberal coasts and the conservative heartland in the middle that U.S. commentator David Brooks wrote about in his "One Nation, Slightly Divisible" article in the December 2001 issue of *The Atlantic Monthly*? Not really.

Many Americans do seem to be clinging to traditional ideas and institutions as anchors in an increasingly chaotic world—and perhaps partly as a reaction to the general (rather dystopian) socio-cultural drift. The evidence certainly isn't limited to our own data. After all, a surprising proportion of our neighbours to the south have shown themselves willing to swallow whole national patriarch George W. Bush's simplistic morality tale about some very good people he knows and the very bad "axis of evil" that seeks to destroy them. A certain desire for stability also surely resides in housing trends in the United States, where the 30 August 2001 edition of *The Economist* reports that 47 million people now live in "association-managed communities" and pay \$35 billion in fees annually to ensure that their neighbourhoods are kept shipshape: desirables in, undesirables out, tasteful landscaping—and, of course, gates that don't squeak as they swing shut.

But the portrait that emerges from our data isn't consistent with the usual rhetoric about America's culture war. The culture war is usually cast as a struggle between the nation's stalwart religious conservatives and its aging hippies (the 90s instalment of the 1969 classic movie *Easy Rider*). The former are said to be frothing retrograde rednecks, while the latter are painted as Baby Boomers whose moral relativism and namby-pamby spiritual stews[3] lead to lives of hypocrisy and feel-good uselessness. This latter portrait is, of course, an unflattering caricature of the non-traditional

---

3. In his book *How We Got Here: The 70's,* David Frum refers to "lukewarm syncretic faith [cobbled together] out of bits and pieces of Buddhism, mysticism, and paganism" (p. 158).

personal fulfillment–seekers at the bottom right of the socio-cultural map. Our data show, however, that the lower-right quadrant is occupied by only about a fifth of the U.S. population—and that proportion is actually declining. The group that is growing rapidly is the group that resides in the lower-*left* quadrant of the map, which already makes up over a quarter of the country's population.

It seems, then, that much of the culture war rhetoric has gotten one of the armies wrong. The group against whose cultural pull religious conservatives are struggling is not the aging hippies with their casual Buddhism and blended families, but the nihilistic denizens of the Intensity and Exclusion quadrant with their *Everyday Rage*, their *Acceptance of Violence*, and their general hostility toward the world around them. These findings would discomfit both the liberal progressives *and* the religious moralists. The political war in America is being waged between the upper-left (Status and Security) and lower-right (Idealism and Autonomy) quadrants, with both sides vying for the votes of the nice, "regular" people in the upper-right (Authenticity and Responsibility) quadrant. What few have realized thus far is that the team that's winning the *cultural* war (the one that really matters) isn't even wearing jerseys: the nihilistic lower-left (Exclusion and Intensity) quadrant is the fastest growing group in America, and they don't vote.

The remarkable thing about social change in America is not that so many people are clinging to old ideas and institutions. Indeed, extreme traditionalism among a portion of the population is a predictable reaction to a broad social movement away from hierarchical forms of authority. (Even in postmodernizing Europe, far-right political movements flourish, to a limited degree, on platforms of racism, xenophobia, and disingenuous nostalgia.) When we consider the United States' tradition of religiosity and moralism, coupled with the stress of everyday life in a nation in which crime, poverty, and illness all loom larger than they do in most other industrialized nations, it is not surprising that traditional values emphasizing order and stability should be so prominent.

What is remarkable about social change in America is the society's absolute failure—or refusal—to postmodernize. Nothing is more striking about the socio-cultural portrait of American social values than the country's wholesale retreat from the idealism and fulfillment side of the map. Americans are moving away *en masse* from the trends associated with civic engagement and social and ecological concern. *Everyday Ethics* and *Ethical Consumerism* are also falling away. The religious are not migrating into the Authenticity and Responsibility quadrant; the fundamentalist sects that are growing most rapidly are located in the upper-*left* quadrant of our map—a psychographic space more disposed to rigidity and exclusion than to old-style decency and civic-mindedness. And as we have already observed, those who are *not* part of the revival of traditional values are, on the whole, not looking hopefully toward an inclusive, progressive tomorrow either. They are looking for thrills, status, and supremacy in the competitive and often dangerous jungle of the lower-left quadrant. Certainly, some Americans are still planted firmly in the postmodern Idealism and Autonomy quadrant, and most of them aren't going anywhere. But they do not define the future of mainstream American values; they are the idealistic remnant of the Civil Rights, anti–Vietnam War, feminist, and environmental movements. (The fact that the socio-political trail they were blazing in the 1960s was not to be appreciated, let alone adopted, by all of their compatriots was clear even in "the Movement's" headiest moments. Lawrence Welk debuted on American prime-time television in 1968, the year the "revolution" took to the streets. American progressivism has always generated a subsequent reaction.) The lower-right quadrant is getting lonelier and lonelier as the rest of the population drifts left on our socio-cultural map, rejecting the autonomy, flexibility, and openness to diversity and change that other advanced industrial societies have embraced. Those in the lower-right quadrant can only look on as American exceptionalism takes on an increasingly dystopian hue. But for these postmodern Americans, maybe there is a land of promise not so very far away. . . .

two

NORTH AMERICA'S TWO DISTINCT SOCIETIES

*Canada and the United States have reached the point where
we can no longer think of each other as foreign countries.*
—Harry S. Truman, U.S. president, address, joint sitting of
the Canadian Senate and House of Commons, 11 June 1947

*He understands I want to make sure our relations with our most
important neighbour to the north of us, the Canadians, is strong. . . .*
—George W. Bush, reacting to a statement of support for his presidential
bid from "Canadian Prime Minister Jean Poutine"; Poutine's thumbs-up
was relayed to President Bush at a 2000 campaign stop by Canadian
comic and *This Hour Has 22 Minutes* "reporter" Rick Mercer

Canada is the largest country in the world that doesn't exist.
—Richard Rodriguez, American social commentator of Mexican-Indian
descent, commenting on the notion that minority groups overtake majority
groups, in an interview by Neil Bissoondath on TVO's *Markings*, 3 July 1995

IN THE DAYS AND WEEKS FOLLOWING 11 September, Canadians' feelings of sympathy for and solidarity with the United States were expressed
again and again. Canadian firefighters and medical professionals travelled
to New York City to offer assistance to those affected by the terrorist
attacks. Families in Newfoundland opened their homes to fearful and

distraught Americans whose planes had been diverted into Canada after news of the disaster had spread through airline communication systems. On 14 September, 100,000 Canadians gathered on Parliament Hill to express their grief over the tragedies that had befallen their neighbours.

The reaction was more immediate and heartfelt than in any other nation. It brought to mind a child in a schoolyard tearfully rushing to the aid of an older sibling in serious distress, affection and fellow feeling blotting out all the usual resentment over quotidian bullying or petty squabbles. Certainly, after things had settled down somewhat, some of the usual fault lines between the two countries began to reappear: Canadians began to wonder about what the U.S. response to the attacks would be, and some eventually began to fret openly (if gingerly) about how Canadians would be drawn into the conflict. But for a short time, the differences between Canada and the United States seemed to dissolve.

As the horror receded and daily life slowly resumed, the differences that had seemed so trivial as to be almost non-existent on that Tuesday morning began to reassert themselves little by little. As 2001 wound shakily down and 2002 began, many Canadians once again found themselves beginning to roll their eyes at phrases like "axis of evil" and shake their heads at George W. Bush's repeated references to the women of Afghanistan as "women of cover." Without losing any of our sympathy for the lives lost or irrevocably altered on 11 September, Canadians began to regain some of their sense of distance and difference from the United States and its worldview.

This slow, tentative process was accelerated very suddenly on 17 April 2002, when news of the deaths of four Canadian soldiers in Afghanistan reached North America (or at least, the news *seemed* to reach North America, but for all the attention it received south of the border it might as well have been lost in transit). The four soldiers were killed (and eight others injured) by "friendly fire"; a U.S. fighter pilot dropped a bomb on the Canadians (whom he mistook for enemy soldiers) as they were carrying out a training exercise on the ground.

"Accidents happen in wars," all voices seemed to concede sadly. "Nobody wanted this to happen." But as President Bush made his first, second, third, fourth, and fifth public appearances the next day without ever mentioning the incident—and even ignoring a question shouted by a Canadian reporter as Bush scuttled away from one press conference— sadness turned to anger. Was it really too much to expect that the United States might have been saddened at having killed and wounded a group of young Canadians who were doing their best to help America fight its war? Was it too much to expect that the American president would at least *pretend* to be dismayed, expressing at least some modest words of empathy and regret? Or that the *New York Times* might have spared a little space somewhere ahead of page fourteen on the day following the incident?

Now Canadians were beginning to recall the old simmering resentments of life in Uncle Sam's backyard. Though the feeling of fraternity that had permeated the country in the period immediately following September 11 had been entirely genuine, this familiar feeling of ill use was no less so. Canadians seemed to recall, in April of 2002, that although it may sometimes seem that Canada and the U.S. are "on the same page," that's usually because we're reading over their shoulder.

Because the cultural differences between Canada and the United States tend to exist beneath the consciousness of our daily lives, it is sometimes possible to imagine that those differences do not exist. After all, on any given day, most Canadians, like most Americans, can be spotted in their natural habitats driving cars, consuming too much energy and water, spending a little less time with their nuclear families than they would like, working a little more than is healthy, watching television, and buying some things they could probably survive without. But differences—both subtle and marked—do exist, and do endure. Some are external (gun control, bilingualism, health care), but many exist only inside the minds of Canadians and Americans—in how they see the world, how they engage with it, and how they hope to shape it.

In the foregoing chapter, I gave a broad outline of the direction of social change in the United States. In this chapter, I will offer a closer look at Canadians' and Americans' responses to individual survey questions— responses that attest, one by one, to a broad trend of cultural *divergence*. Subsequently, we will place Canada and the United States in the same socio-cultural mapspace, so that we can see how the two countries' trajectories of social change appear relative to one another when they're placed in the same graphic territory.

But before the big picture, I'd like to share some raw numbers. We begin our portrait of these two neighbours with a comparison of their religious convictions. Canadians are by now quite familiar with evangelists Jerry Falwell, Pat Robertson, Jimmy Swaggart, Jim and Tammy Faye Bakker (who are slowly getting back to the business), and even William Jennings Bryan, who defended creationism in the famous Scopes Monkey trial in the 1920s. We know that Christian fundamentalism has far deeper and more enduring roots in the United States, particularly in the Bible Belt, than here in Canada. What we sometimes fail to remember is that not so long ago, Canadians were more conventionally religious than Americans. In the mid-1950s, 60 per cent of Canadians told pollsters they went to church each Sunday; the proportion in the U.S. at that time was only 50 per cent. Today, only a fifth of Canadians claim weekly church attendance (22 per cent, according to Ekos), whereas the proportion in the U.S. is 42 per cent. A 2002 Pew Research Center poll found religion to be important to 59 per cent of Americans—the highest proportion in all the developed nations surveyed—and to only 30 per cent of Canadians, a rate similar to that found in Great Britain and Italy. Nearly four in ten Canadians do not consider themselves to be members of a religious faith. In the U.S. the proportion of atheists, agnostics, or secular humanists is only 25 per cent. In less than a generation, Canadians have evolved from being much more religious than Americans to being considerably less so.

Canadians have not only rejected in large numbers the authority of religious institutions, but have brought this questioning of traditional authority closer to home. Our research shows Canadians to be far less likely than Americans to agree with the statement, "The father of the family must be master in his own home." In 1992 we found that 26 per cent of Canadians believed Father must be master (down from 42 per cent in 1983). In 1992, 42 per cent of Americans told us Dad should be on top. Since then the gap has widened: down to 20 per cent in Canada and up to 44 per cent in the U.S. in 1996, and then down even further (to 18

per cent) in Canada in 2000 and up further still (to 49 per cent) in the
U.S. in that year. The widening gap between the two countries now
stands at an astonishing thirty-one points, with Canadians becoming ever
less deferential to patriarchal authority and Americans becoming more
and more willing to Wait Till Their Father Comes Home to find out if it's
okay to watch *The Simpsons*.

**Father of Family Must be Master in His Own House
Canada and the United States: Agree 1992, 1996, & 2000**

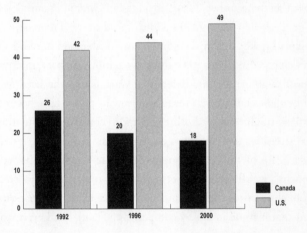

Paralleling this differing orientation to patriarchal authority are the
two populations' attitudes toward the relative status of the sexes. In a
word, Americans are more predisposed to male chauvinism than
Canadians, and here again the gap is widening. In 1992, 26 per cent of
Canadians told us that men are naturally superior to women, while 30 per
cent of Americans felt the same way. Four years later in 1996, the proportion of Canadians believing in the innate superiority of men declined to
23 per cent while the U.S. proportion rose to 32 per cent. By 2000, the
proportion in Canada stood at 24 per cent while that in the U.S. shot up
to 38 per cent. It only stands to reason, many Americans seem to be
telling us, that if God-fearing men are the superior beings on this planet,
then they should certainly be the bosses in their own homes.

Canadians' more egalitarian views regarding the status of women and the structure of the family, plus a more skeptical view of traditional institutional authority, also seem to lead them to a more relaxed view of what constitutes a family. Over the past decade, Canadians have consistently felt that two people living together, what we used to call living common-law, in fact constitutes a family. In 2000, 71 per cent of Canadians felt a couple that shared a home were a family, up from 66 per cent in 1992. Only 54 per cent of Americans shared this view, albeit up from 49 per cent in 1992. It is almost impossible to imagine a governor of any U.S. state daring to brazenly "live in sin" with his or her "life partner" as can Ontario Premier Ernie Eves. When in 1942 the Conservatives added the adjective "Progressive" to their party name, I doubt they had common-law cohabitation in mind.

What emerges so far is a portrait of two nations evolving in unexpected directions: the once shy and deferential Canadians, who used to wait to be told by their betters what to do and how to think, have become more skeptical of traditional authority and more confident about their own personal decisions and informal arrangements. Americans, by contrast, seeking a little of the "peace and order" that Canadians hoped "good government" would provide, seem inclined to latch on to traditional institutional practices, beliefs, and norms as anchors in a national environment that is more intensely competitive, chaotic, and even violent.

Attitudes toward violence are, in fact, among the features that most markedly differentiate Canadians from Americans. In the year 2000, 50 per cent of Canadians told us they felt violence to be all around them, a high figure to be sure, but nowhere near the 76 per cent of Americans who felt the same way. Americans' responses to our questions about violence suggest that they may even be becoming inured to the violence they perceive to be ubiquitous. In 1992, 9 per cent of Canadians and 10 per cent of Americans told us that violence is a normal part of life, nothing to be concerned about. In 1996, the figure in Canada was still 9 per cent, but had grown to 18 per cent in the U.S. In 2000, 12 per cent of Canadians felt that violence in everyday life was normal, but in the same year 24 per cent of Americans felt the same way. For one American in four, representing 70 million people, violence is perceived as a normal part of one's daily routine. The other three-quarters of the population, presumably, are doing all they can to avoid those 70 million, particularly if alone on the street after dark.

We found further evidence that violence is becoming more, not less, normative in America when we asked Americans to agree or disagree that when one is extremely tense or frustrated, a little violence can offer relief, and that "it's no big deal." In 1992, 14 per cent of Americans agreed with this sentiment, as did 14 per cent of Canadians we polled. In 1996, the proportion was 10 per cent in Canada but zoomed to 27 per cent in the U.S. By 2000, the proportion in Canada was back up to 14 per cent, but had surged further to 31 per cent in America, nearly one-third of the population. Again, you might not want to confront one of these folks when they're feeling a bit on edge, particularly when you remember that many of them (including the U.S. Attorney General) believe their Constitution guarantees them the right to bear firearms.

America is and always has been a very competitive society, nurtured by the myth of the American Dream, which suggests that anyone with a little vision and a lot of hard work can achieve material success. Sociologist Seymour Martin Lipset points out that in all categories, crime rates in America are about three times higher than they are in other industrialized countries. Lipset suggests as an explanation for this phenomenon the following: the American Dream, and the concomitant imperative to achieve material success, are so strong in America that many people pursue the goals of wealth and status in reckless, sometimes even criminal, ways. The end is of such monumental importance that the means become almost irrelevant.

Our polling found some interesting results in this area. In 1992, we asked Canadians and Americans whether they would be prepared to take "great risks" in order to get what they want. That year, nearly equal proportions of Canadians (25 per cent) and Americans (26 per cent) reported that they would indeed be prepared to take great risks to get what they wanted. The same in 1996. But by 2000 still only a quarter of Canadians were prepared to take great risks while the proportion in the U.S. increased to 38 per cent—a full eleven points higher than in Canada.

Americans are prepared to put a lot more on the line than Canadians to achieve their version of the American Dream, including personal risks to life and limb. They are also, as it turns out, more willing than Canadians to risk the lives and limbs of others to achieve the same ends. In 1992, 10 per cent of Canadians and only 9 per cent of Americans told us that it is acceptable to use violence to get what you want. In 1996, 11 per cent of Canadians felt this way, but the proportion of Americans rose to 17 per cent. By 2000, 13 per cent of Canadians felt the use of violence, presumably on or off the ice, was an acceptable way of achieving one's objectives, while the proportion in the U.S. was 23 per cent, nearly one in four and almost double the figure in Canada.

Lipset's hypothesis about the possible relationship between crime and the deep-rooted imperative of the American Dream illuminates an interesting contradiction: frustrated by their inability to achieve the Dream by socially acceptable means, those who obtain the trappings of success unlawfully exercise excessive individualism precisely *in order* to conform.

The idea that America's ostensible commitment to individualism may mask a deep impulse toward conformity is borne out in our polling data. We find that Americans are in fact more prone to conformity than their neighbours to the north, who reside in a land that not only tolerates but actually celebrates linguistic, ethnic, and regional group identities. We track three items that shed light on this intriguing question: do people mind changing their habits, do they relate to people who show originality in dress and behaviour, and do they relate to people who repress rather than show their emotions. Our findings are surprising. In 1992, 51 per cent of Canadians and 56 per cent of Americans reported that they did not like changing their habits. In 1996, 48 per cent of Canadians reported being stuck in their ways—a decline of three points—and 58 per cent of Americans said the same thing, an increase of two points. By 2000, we had a widening and quite significant gap: only 42 per cent of Canadians said they don't like changing their habits while 54 per cent of Americans reported the same, now a gap of twelve points showing Canadians to be less conservative and more flexible than Americans in their day-to-day routines.

How about conformity of dress and behaviour: wearing the right costume or uniform for the occasion, not saying or doing anything politically incorrect? Who are the conformists? Who are the rebels? In 1992, 1996, and 2000 a consistent two-thirds of Canadians (68, 68, and 67 per cent) told us that they relate to nonconformists. Conversely, in each year, the proportion of Americans who do so dropped: from 64 per cent in 1992 to 61 per cent in 1996 to 52 per cent in 2000. Overall, the gap between the U.S. and Canada stands at 15 per cent. That George W. Bush, after his election, instantly reinstated a strict suit-and-tie dress code at the White House illustrates this penchant for order and decorum, in stark contrast to the Clinton-era "wonk casual" image. Meanwhile, Canada's male politicians go out of their way to dress informally, almost invariably replacing their blue suits with open-collared sports shirts when on the campaign trail. One of the truly remarkable silent social revolutions in Canada has been the rapid death of the dress code. Dress-down Friday became dress-down every day in the Canadian workplace in a matter of months. In New York many upscale restaurants still strictly enforce a jacket-and-tie dress code; in Toronto only the stuffiest of private clubs have a store of apparel for the uncouth who show up improperly attired.

And finally, what about emotional informality and openness? Who are more open: the famously friendly "y'all come back real soon" Americans or the reputedly reserved, understated (even cold?) Canadians? In 1992, 32 per cent of Canadians told us that they relate best to people who do not show their emotions. In 1996 we found a similar proportion (28 per cent), and in 2000 30 per cent—essentially no change over the decade. In 1992, the proportion of Americans who preferred the stiff-upper-lip type was 27 per cent—five points lower than in Canada, as expected. But in 1996 that proportion rose to 35 per cent, and then in 2000 shot up even further to 44 per cent—an astounding fourteen-point gap. It's hard to get your head around the idea of a touchy-feely Canadian in contrast to the emotionally restrained, uptight American. But think back—way back— to the strong, silent heroes of American westerns who let their guns do the talking and held their liquor as if it were Ovaltine. The late 90s have seen a tremendous backlash in the U.S. against the earlier trend toward "feminization." Today that forgotten cowboy, the one who doesn't have much time for fancy language or womanish diplomacy but sure knows what to do with an axis of evil when he sees one, is back in style.

Soon after 9/11, President George Bush and then New York Mayor Rudolph Giuliani urged Americans to demonstrate their patriotism in defiance of the forces of evil who "wish to destroy our way of life." The president and the mayor urged their fellow Americans to go out shopping. This the people did, thus saving the U.S. (and Canada) from recession. These leaders knew they were addressing receptive audiences: hordes of people who not only felt a genuine desire to do something, anything, to respond to those deeply traumatic events in a helpful way, but who had also been weaned on the idea that material possessions are among the most important expressions of one's status, interests, personality, and citizenship in the greatest country on earth. In 1992, 38 per cent of Americans told us it was important that people admire the things they own. Similar proportions in 1996 (37 per cent) and 2000 (36 per cent) said the same thing. In Canada, meanwhile, ostentatious consumption has been in gentle decline: from 34 per cent in 1992, to 32 percent in 1996, and down to 29 per cent in 2000. Many Canadians are still conspicuous consumers, but they lag behind their American cousins and seem to be drifting away from consuming "things" toward enjoying "experience." Americans brag about the new car they just bought; Canadians are more likely to boast about the trips they have taken.

"I figure if I don't have that third Martini, then the terrorists win."

Given Americans' greater orientation to consumption, together with their greater confidence in institutional authorities, it should not be surprising that they take greater pleasure in (and trust more) the promises of Madison Avenue. In 1992, 34 per cent of Canadians told us that they derived great pleasure from looking at advertising. But that proportion declined slightly in subsequent surveys to 30 per cent in 1996 and 29 per cent in 2000. Just the opposite happened in the United States. In 1992, 38 per cent of Americans said they got great pleasure out of advertising. This increased to 40 per cent in 1996 and 41 per cent in 2000, leaving a gap of twelve points between Canada and the U.S.

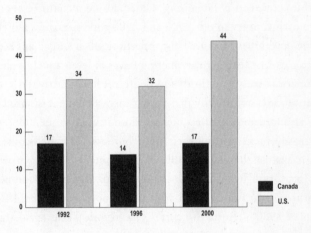

A Widely Advertised Product Is Probably Good
Canada and the United States – Agree 1992, 1996 & 2000

When asked in 1992 if they believed that a widely advertised product was probably a good product, 17 per cent of Canadians said yes. In 1996, 14 per cent said yes. And in 2000 again 17 per cent said yes. In other words, more than eight in ten Canadians are skeptical of the claims of advertisers, which may explain why humour, irony, and even self-deprecation go down better than the hard sell in cynical Canada. In the U.S., we see dramatically different results. In 1992, 34 per cent of Americans told us that a widely advertised product is probably a good one. A similar proportion agreed in 1996 (32 per cent), but in 2000 the figure shot up to 44 per cent, leaving a gap of fully twenty-seven points between Americans and Canadians. Hats off to Joe Canadian, then: it seems that a successful ad targeted at Canadians is truly a remarkable achievement.

Public health insurance is an important reason why Canada spends more than 40 per cent of its gross domestic product (GDP) in the public sector while the U.S. is closer to 30 per cent. From World War II until the 1980s the role of government grew steadily in Canada, and the public sector has since more or less maintained its share of GDP. The same was true in the United States: growth of government through the 1970s, followed in the 1980s and 1990s with more or less stable expenditures, although the 1996 Welfare Reform went a long way toward revoking what had been an entitlement in that country since Franklin Roosevelt's New Deal in the 1930s.

In this context, it is interesting that equal proportions of about one-third in each country in our 1996 and 2000 surveys express a preference for more government involvement. At a time when Canadians are being taxed to pay for existing government services at levels much higher than their American cousins, a third of us desire a still *more* active government. By contrast, it is noteworthy that more Americans, the least taxed people in the advanced industrial economies, do not wish to see more government involvement within their own borders. The neo-conservative backlash against the growing role of government that began with the 1970s "Sagebrush Rebellion"—including the passage of anti–property tax Proposition 13 in California in 1978 and capped with Ronald Reagan's election in 1980—returns America to its historical bias against government activism. Less than one in three Americans wishes for a change in the generally laissez-faire approach of U.S. government, whereas Canada and Europe remain largely dedicated to the preservation of the social welfare state. The sustainability of the tax gap between the United States and Canada is one of the most intriguing challenges of Canadian public policy, but one that is not under serious threat by the forces of Canadian neo-conservatism. Theoretically, the gap is sustainable if Canadians continue to feel they receive high-quality public services in return for their tax money, and thus enjoy a high *quality of life* even in the face of a relative *standard of living* they are constantly reminded is eroding.

It is interesting to place these attitudes toward government in the context of the comparative sense of social responsibility in the two countries. Americans are said to be the most generous people on earth, given their high rates of philanthropy and volunteerism. Canadians do fewer such good deeds voluntarily, but have a compulsory philanthropic mechanism known as taxes (which most people support voluntarily at the ballot box in voting for political parties that sustain much higher levels of public spending in this country).

Setting aside, for the moment, the different means by which we go about helping others, what are the basic orientations to the plight of the less well off on each side of the border? In 1996 and again in 2000 we asked Canadians and Americans if they felt a personal responsibility to those worse off than themselves. While the proportions are high in each country, more Canadians than Americans expressed a sense of social responsibility in each survey: 72 per cent (Canada) to 70 per cent (U.S.) in 1996 and 70 per cent (Canada) to 65 per cent (U.S.) in 2000. This runs counter to the myth of stingy Canadians versus generous Americans. Despite the high taxes we pay to support a welfare state, Canadians still feel as much personal responsibility to the less well off as do the less taxed, more affluent, and more conventionally religious Americans. Canadians don't take a dismissive "I gave at the office" attitude toward those in need of assistance, even though they did in fact give at the office in most cases, with large portions of their paycheques being lopped off at the source for the taxman, not to mention the plethora of user fees and other taxes Canadians pay, including that on goods and services purchased.

And as it turns out, Canadians' road to heaven is not just paved with good intentions. According to the Canadian Centre for Philanthropy,[1] 88 per cent of Canadians made financial or in-kind donations to charitable and non-profit organizations in 1997. This compares with the 70 per cent of American households (representing probably a lower percentage of individuals) that did so in 1998. Americans direct relatively more of their support to religious organizations, while the more secular Canadians donate relatively more to health and social service organizations.

---

1. *Research Bulletin* vol. 7, nos. 2 and 3.

Our surveys show Americans to be engaged in an increasingly frenetic struggle to maintain a standard of living that is measured almost solely by material possessions. The proportion of Americans telling us they are having trouble accomplishing things due to a hectic life increased from 80 per cent in 1992 to 83 per cent in 2000, while the proportion of Canadians saying the same actually dropped from 75 per cent in 1992 to 68 per cent in 2000—a Canada–U.S. gap of fifteen points. Another measure of the relative stress Americans are feeling in keeping up with the Joneses is their increasing need for personal escape. In 1992, 58 per cent of Americans reported that it was important to them to get away from the responsibilities and burdens of their lives, a proportion that grew to 63 per cent in 2000. In Canada, the proportion reporting the same need for respite declined from 54 per cent in 1992 to 50 per cent in 2000— leaving a thirteen-point gap between Americans and Canadians.

"So many toys—so little unstructured time."

Data gathered by the International Labour Organization[2] shows that from 1980 to 2000, actual average working hours per American adult (aged fifteen to sixty-four) rose by 234 hours from 1,242 to 1,476, an

2. Lars Osberg, "Time, Money and Inequality in International Perspective," 28 November 2002.

increase of 19 per cent, representing another five forty-hour weeks of work each year. In the same period, starting from a similar base as the Americans, Canadians worked only another forty hours a year, representing only another week and a half of work per year. In the meantime, Germans worked 170 hours less than they did twenty years earlier while still managing to produce some of the best cars in the world.

The Europeans cling to their six- to eight-week vacation allotments, savouring their leisure, while Canadians, feeling that the Europeans have figured it out, cringe in guilt as yet another right-wing think tank tells them they are a bunch of lazy sots who should pick up their socks and get back to work if they don't wish to fall even further behind their American cousins. No wonder stress has become the disease in America that dares not speak its name.

In his 2002 book *Wealth and Democracy,* Kevin Phillips provides more than a few clues as to why Americans work more and are more stressed than Canadians. Phillips's 428-page, statistics-laden tome provides plenty of evidence as to why the quest for the American Dream has been particularly stressful south of the border. He documents the astounding gap between the rich and the poor in America on measures of both income and wealth, quoting a 1999 *New York Times* article that reports the stunning new truth: "The gap between rich and poor has grown into an economic chasm so wide that this year the richest 2.7 million Americans, the top one per cent, will have as many after-tax dollars to spend as the bottom 100 million" (p. 103). Between 1979 and 1989, the portion of the nation's wealth held by the top 1 per cent nearly doubled, skyrocketing from 22 per cent to 39 per cent, the most rapid escalation in U.S. history. Phillips usefully contrasts the incomes of middle-class Americans in the period after World War II to that of the boom times of the 1980s and 90s. Whereas in the postwar period it was the middle class whose incomes were increasing the most rapidly, by 1999 the average real after-tax income of the middle 60 per cent of the population in the U.S. was lower than in 1977. The bottom 20 per cent were dramatically worse off, while only the top 20 per cent of income earners found themselves to be among the happy few who were better off. In comparing America with the rest of the developed world, Phillips concludes that in a little over two centuries, the United States has evolved from an egalitarian democracy to the country with the largest gap of wealth and incomes between the rich and the poor, and, parenthetically, now has a political system essentially for sale to the highest bidder. In such a setting, two-breadwinner households working longer hours with deteriorating job benefits and job security, and with lengthier commutes to those insecure jobs, are paying a huge price in terms of the stress of competing in a race most are destined to lose.

These pressures of course are also evident in Canada, but as usual much less so. Canada has witnessed a slightly growing gap between the rich and others, but evidence gathered by Statistics Canada shows little change in the income distribution over the past twenty years, thanks in part to transfers from the state (rich taxpayers) to the less well off, and "free" access to public services like medicare. In an August 2000 article in Statistics Canada's *Canadian Economic Observer,* economists Michael Wolfson and Brian Murphy found that, as of 1997, the poorest 25 per cent of Canadian families were better off than their U.S. counterparts in terms of purchasing power. Those Americans in the top fifth of the income spectrum, however, have disposable incomes 25 per cent higher than their Canadian peers.

The data show that the richest Canadians are not as well off financially as equivalent Americans, while the poorest Canadians are infinitely better off than their counterparts south of the border. All of which proves, at least in terms of income, that it's better to be poor in Canada and rich in America.

"The implication," according to Wolfson and Murphy, "is that Canada and the U.S. have remained socially and politically distinct with regard to the forces and government policies shaping income distribution. Notwithstanding the open border, these differences have had greater impacts than economic forces." The authors conclude, "The 49th parallel does seem to matter" (p. 322).

Of course, Canada does have its very rich. In a draft article entitled "The Evolution of High Incomes in Canada, 1920–2000," professor Michael Veall and his colleague Emmanuel Saez find the top 1 per cent of Canadian income earners to be every bit as well off relative to the total population of their county as are their American counterparts. Part of the reason seems to be an increasingly continental market, not just for professional athletes but also for top executives, especially since these people are so mobile and so many firms in Canada are U.S.-owned in the first place. In these circles, language and culture (for non-francophones) are no barrier; these super-rich North Americans constitute an increasingly transnational subculture, as comfortable at work on Wall Street as on Bay Street, and at play in Nantucket as in Muskoka.

This elite is in the vanguard of the Canadian neo-conservative mindset. They move in a world of their own, one in which the public domain is almost completely supplanted by the private. The very rich have no need of government insurance or public transfers to help them in case of loss of employment or old age. They have replaced protection by local police with private security systems and services, and if public medicare becomes too much of a nuisance, they use their who-you-know network to jump the queue or shoot down to the Mayo Clinic for speedy service. At the slightest hint that the local public school can't provide one-on-one tutoring for Junior struggling with his arithmetic and spelling, they have him enrolled in a private school faster than you can write a cheque.

In this exalted world, the public services for everyone, which go a long way in defining the difference between Canada and the United States, become almost completely irrelevant. These people in effect divorce their country and join the continental boardroom and country club, most prominently exemplified by former prime minister Brian Mulroney, for whom Canada's highest elective office has proven to be a stepping stone to better opportunities south of the border.

While this happy few in the top 1 per cent of our business elite may have an increasingly transnational mindset, Canadian tax policy forces the remainder of the country's middle class to subsidize the poor and support Canada's version of the social welfare state, something most of them do quite willingly.

Our surveys looked at another issue related to social cohesion and governance: civic engagement. American political scientist Robert Putnam has become famous for his best-selling 2000 book *Bowling Alone,* in which he documents the rapid decline in participation in social and civic life in America. Our data support Putnam's thesis, at least for the United States.

In 1992, 1996, and 2000 we asked Americans and Canadians if they discuss local problems and issues with other people. In 1992, two-thirds of Americans (66 per cent) said they did so, a much higher proportion than we found in Canada (52 per cent). In 1996, the proportion in Canada was about the same as in 1992 (50 per cent), but had dropped to 53 per cent in the U.S. By 2000, the proportion in Canada stood at 47 per cent, representing a mild erosion over the previous decade. However, in the U.S. we found the proportion to have plummeted to only 34 per cent— down a whopping thirty-two points from the 66 per cent who were engaged in 1992. If our data and Putnam's vast assembly of statistics are correct, the 1990s witnessed a sea change in the level of civic engagement in America. The entire society seems to have retreated from community involvement into private fortified worlds into which each family member escapes into the fantasy of individualized multimedia diversions. With the combined stress of working longer hours with longer commutes, and the retreat into the virtual worlds of television and now the Web, no wonder there is little time left for the PTA, the Little League, and good old-fashioned neighbouring. Canadians may be getting there too, but if so they are moving much more slowly in that direction.

**Discuss Local Problems with People
Canada and the United States: Agree 1992, 1996, & 2000**

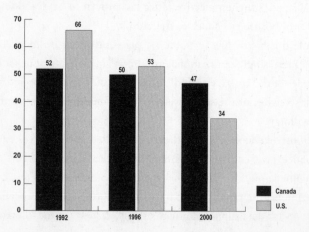

Putnam finds that by the 1990s television was absorbing almost 40 per cent of the average American's leisure time, a third more than in the 1960s, for a total of four hours per day, or twenty-eight hours per week (p. 222). Moreover, Putnam reports that the fraction of sixth-graders with a TV set in their bedroom grew from 6 per cent in 1970 to 77 per cent in 1999, and that two American kids in three aged eight to eighteen say that the TV is usually on during meals in their home.

Canadian media consultant Barry Kiefl, in a paper delivered to the Professional Market Research Society in June 2000 that cites AC Neilsen, B.B.M., and Statistics Canada data, shows the equivalent television viewing figures for Canadians to be about a quarter less than the U.S. numbers: just over three hours a day, or twenty-two hours per week. This proportion has changed little from readings in the late 1960s. Canadians love their televisions too, but their addiction seems to have taken a much less serious toll on family interaction and civic engagement than is the case in the United States.

Another indicator of the diverging lifestyles of Americans and Canadians is the comparative statistics on body mass. According to the U.S. National Center for Health Statistics' 1999/2000 National Health and Nutrition Examination Survey and Statistics Canada's 2000/2001 Canadian Community Health Survey, 65 per cent of Americans, as compared with 48 per cent of Canadians, are overweight. When it comes to the more health-threatening status of obesity, the proportion in the U.S. is 31 per cent, whereas in Canada it's only 15 per cent. Of course, obesity is the consequence of a variety of factors, not the least of which is one's socio-economic status. Lower-income people are less likely than those with higher incomes to eat nutritious foods and are more likely to lead sedentary lives than the better off.

One explanation could be that the poorest Canadians, as we have seen, are relatively better off than their American peers, but even this significant factor cannot explain why Americans are nearly twice as likely as Canadians to be obese. Nor does ethnic composition (America having more groups prone to obesity) or other demographic differences entirely explain the disparity. Nor do differences in climate (Canadians burning off calories in their cold winter). The answer, I believe, is to be found in the combination of all these many factors, but more important is the fact that the two countries have evolved different hierarchies of values in which relatively greater numbers of Canadians have a sense of autonomy and personal control, including control over their own bodies.

The final battery of trends we have tracked deals with some broader societal issues. We start out with nationalism, remembering that our surveys took place prior to 9/11. In each country we asked respondents if they enjoyed showing foreigners how much smarter and stronger "we" are than "they." Reflecting our increasingly modest place in this planet, it is not surprising that only 17 per cent of Canadians in 1992 said they enjoyed demonstrating Canadian superiority, a proportion that dropped to 16 per cent in 1996 and further to 14 per cent in 2000. (I was not granted the opportunity to participate in any of these surveys.) Not surprisingly, the numbers in the U.S. are much higher: 27 per cent in 1992, 23 per cent in 1996, and back up to 31 per cent in 2000. A post-9/11 sampling would surely be higher still.

Each of these countries is a land of immigrants or the descendents of immigrants. Each is becoming increasingly multicultural, but not equally enamoured of its multicultural and multiracial diversity. This should not be surprising if we remember the history of slavery and continuing racism in American society; the former of which Canada was, for the most part, thankfully spared. In 1992, 1996, and 2000 we asked respondents in Canada and the U.S. to agree or disagree with the statement "Non-whites should not be allowed to immigrate to this country." In 1992 only 11 per cent of Canadians thought so. The same proportion was found in 1996, and in 2000 it was 13 per cent. Over the same period in America the proportions rose steadily from 16 per cent in 1992 to 23 per cent in 1996 to 25 per cent in 2000. At the turn of the millennium, we can say that by this measure one in ten Canadians is overtly racist as is one in four Americans, and the trend in the U.S. is not good. Again, these are the results of pre-9/11 samplings, although a subsequent 2002 Pew Research Center poll of more than 38,000 people in 44 countries found Canada to be the only nation where a majority, in this case a very strong majority of 77 per cent, said that immigrants have a good influence on their country, well ahead of the United States where only 49 per cent felt the same way. Forty-three per cent of Americans said that immigrants were bad for their nation, more than double the proportion of Canadians (18 per cent) who had a negative view of newcomers in their country.

In America, xenophobia has been given recent political expression in the presidential campaigns of Ross Perot and Pat Buchanan, the former being credited with taking enough votes from the Republicans in 1992 and 1996 to help elect and re-elect Bill Clinton, the latter labelling Canada "Soviet Canuckistan" in 2002 for not quickly and vigorously toeing the American government's foreign policy line. In Canada, political parties, even on the right of the ideological spectrum, are careful to avoid any whiff of xenophobia or racism. MPs who wade into this dangerous territory, even with pathetic attempts at humour, find themselves quickly chastised and their careers in public life precipitously terminated.

On a case-by-case basis, these survey numbers are interesting and probably surprising to many. In aggregate, they indicate a divergence in Canadians' and Americans' values that is truly amazing, given all the experiences and influences the two countries hold in common. It's not unusual for a Canadian to express that he or she *feels* different from American friends, colleagues, or even relatives; it is unusual, however, to see this feeling quantified.

In the realm of the mass media, the past several decades have witnessed a trend toward greater tolerance of sex and coarse language and, more recently, even of violence on mainstream television in Canada—both in programs broadcast and in commercial advertising. Soft-core pornography has been aired for late-night viewing in Toronto since Moses Znaimer debuted the Friday night Baby Blue movie on CityTV in 1972. Not to be outdone, Quebecers also enjoy the titillation of their own soft-core porn in TQS's Bleu Nuit offerings. Such fare is certainly available on American television, but, with the exception of "Midnight Blue" in New York City, only for those willing to pay for specialty cable and satellite offerings. The smash hit *The Sopranos*, for example, is available in the U.S. only through Time Warner's Home Box Office (HBO), while the same program featuring over-the-top nudity, violence, and coarse language is broadcast in Canada over the regular CTV network (the only restriction the Canadian Broadcast Standards Council has imposed on the show is that it be aired after 9:00 p.m.).

Canada's increasing tolerance of content offensive to some viewers contrasts with the growing power of conservative religious minorities in the U.S. to influence advertisers and broadcast regulators to ban material deemed to be offensive. Incidentally, most of these same censors are staunch supporters of the right of Americans to bear arms, but in opposing bare arms they reveal their views on violence and nudity to be roughly opposite those of most Canadians.

Another everyday expression of the widening gap between American and Canadian values is the relative size of the market for minivans and sport-utility vehicles in each country. The automobile has become one of the most potent symbols of one's personal image and place in the status hierarchy in modern countries. In no country is this truer than in the United States, and in no region of the U.S. is this truer than in Southern California. In the research that Environics has done, the minivan is found to be symbolic of familism, an acceptance that children and their world are now at the centre of one's life. Nothing is more important to North American minivan owners than being viewed as good moms and dads, and nothing gives them greater personal pleasure than picking up their kids from school or soccer practice, secure in the knowledge that there is plenty of room for Junior and Sis's buddies in the spacious and safe cocoon of a child-friendly minivan. Minivan owners are also savvy bargain hunters, looking to stretch their dollars as far as they can, and dollar for dollar, nothing beats the value and versatility of a minivan. Few look for anything fancy in their minivans (apart from a DVD monitor playing Barney videos to keep the kids quiet on trips to Grandma's), and most would agree that a car is just an appliance for getting from A to B, rather than something that reflects their personalities or social standing.

"You just parked on a Saturn."

The SUV owner, on the other hand, is, or at least aspires to be, a rugged individualist who can navigate with equal ease the dangers of the Sonoran Desert and more probably the (sub)urban jungle. For these owners, buying a minivan would mean forever being confined to the drudgery of suburbia and an acceptance that life is no longer an adventure. The fact that most SUV owners use their vehicles no differently from minivan owners, and that the most serious off-roading they ever see are the speed bumps in the local Home Depot parking lot, does not dissuade hundreds of thousands of SUV buyers every year. The SUV brilliantly appeals to Americans' other-directed individualism, and no more so than in Los Angeles, where the latest craze to be adopted by Hollywood celebrities like Fred Durst of Limp Bizkit and actor Brad Pitt is the Mercedes-Benz G500 SUV, a gentrified version of a former military vehicle in a pattern similar to the transformation of the eponymous Jeep into an urban assault vehicle more than a decade ago. Because so few units have been sold, the G500 is a perfect symbol of Los Angelenos' renowned penchant for conspicuous consumption (although one can already sense the imminent loss of its cool "It" edge with talk of a redesigned Hummer H2—of the 1990 Persian Gulf Desert Storm fame—the prototype of which "buzz marketers" will undoubtedly lend to Arnold Schwarzenegger for his gubernatorial campaign in an effort to introduce Californians to yet another trendy toy).

Now being bought by Boomers who once embraced Doyle Dane's brilliant "Think Small" campaign for Volkswagen in the 1960s, SUVs are experiencing a backlash in America that is reminiscent of the anti-fur campaign in the 1980s and 1990s. Environmental groups are slapping fake tickets charging the vehicle owners with excessive gasoline consumption, pollution, and safety violations. Meanwhile, owners and manufacturers alike fiercely defend Americans' rights to buy whatever they want.

In Canada, minivans outsell SUVs by a ratio of two to one. In the United States, SUVs outsell minivans two to one. This is a stark difference whose roots can be traced directly to the differing values of our two countries.

WE ARE EXTREMELY FORTUNATE to have a large repository of comparable data for Canada and the United States which measures the socio-cultural phenomena that underlie differences in television fare and monster vehicle ownership. The items I sketched above are only some of the questions to which we have responses from both Canadians and Americans. It's fairly interesting to look at these questions even in isolation—much as we see single polling items in daily newspapers, raise our eyebrows, and in most cases promptly forget them. But what is truly fascinating is to see how these data, in aggregate, allow us to not only plot the two societies' positions on their respective social values mapspaces, but to actually compare their trajectories of social change. (I am fond of reminding my colleagues that "two points make a hypothesis but three points make a story." In this case, our three points are 1992, 1996, and 2000, the years in which we conducted our surveys throughout North America.) After all, if the questions we asked Canadians and Americans are comparable on an individual level, then the stories their responses generate on our socio-cultural maps are also comparable. The result is an empirically based graphic representation of the two countries' paths of social change:

quite literally, a *picture* of the hotly debated convergence with or divergence from Canada's neighbours to the south.

Before turning to that remarkable picture our data yield when seen through the lens of the Environics social values tracking tool, it's necessary to offer a word about the map itself. As I stressed in the preceding chapter, the socio-cultural map of a given sample is generated by the kinds of answers respondents in that sample give to our questions, and how those answers correlate with one another. As a result, different societies produce, and are in turn plotted onto, socio-cultural maps that differ in their axes and the positioning on the map of the values tracked. We will see an example of this phenomenon in this book: Canada's social values map (described in Appendix F) is slightly different from that of the United States.

In order to compare the two countries' trajectories of social change, we need to place them in a common landscape. As my colleagues and I sought to produce this common landscape, there were three choices available to us: plot both countries on the Canadian map, plot both countries on the U.S. map, or generate a single North American map whose axes and layout would be determined by the data gathered from *all* respondents, both Canadian and American.

At first glance, the third option seems the obvious choice. But creating a North American map is not without its difficulties, chief of which results from the population differential between the two societies. If we were to create a common North American map weighting all respondents equally, as we did for each of the single-nation maps, then the whole exercise would be futile. Because the population of the U.S. is roughly ten times that of Canada, the North American map would be so strongly skewed to reflect the U.S. socio-cultural landscape that it would be virtually identical to the U.S. map. If, however, we were to create a North American map weighting Canada and the U.S. equally (that is, assigning ten times the importance to each Canadian respondent as compared with each U.S. respondent), we would create a skew of another kind, and the map would not accurately reflect the relationship between the two countries' trajectories.

Ultimately, my data-crunching colleagues and I decided that, for the sake of both accuracy and simplicity of explanation (how rare that those two criteria demand the same solution), it would be best to plot Canada passively on the U.S. map. When I say "passively," I mean that Canadians' responses to our questions are *not* used in the calculations that bring about the construction of the map itself; they are just used to situate Canada within the American socio-cultural landscape. That is, Canada's three points (1992, 1996, and 2000) are plotted onto the pre-existing U.S. map.

So, in plotting Canada passively onto the U.S. map, we are essentially treating Canadians as a subset of the U.S. population: we plot Canadians just as we might plot American married men, Asian-Americans, American women with post-secondary education, or any other group. The only difference is that the survey responses of members of the three demographic groups just named would have been part of the original stew of data that gave rise to the U.S. map, whereas Canadians were not part of that original stew.

(Note: Canadian readers should make their way to the end of this chapter before they read too much metaphor and portent into all this talk of treating Canadians as a subset of the U.S. population.)

Now that we've established the mapspace in which our comparison of Canada and the U.S. is to be carried out, we can turn our attention to the actual plotting of the two countries' locations in 1992, 1996, and 2000. Since we're using the American map, the plotting of America's three-point story tells us nothing we haven't already seen in Chapter One. In the period from 1992 to 2000 we saw many Americans drifting from the upper-right Authenticity and Responsibility quadrant down and left into the Exclusion and Intensity quadrant. As I discussed more fully in Chapter One, this movement is out of step with social change in most industrialized nations: rather than moving toward greater autonomy, idealism, and inner direction, Americans are moving into an area of the map where we find values of nihilism, aggression, fear of the other, and consumptive one-upmanship.

One look at the Canadian trajectory on the American map should immediately dispel any notion that Canadian social values are becoming indistinguishable from those in the United States. Rather, when we plot the evolution of Canadian social values on the American map, we find a picture of startling dissimilitude, and—even more striking—ongoing divergence. Not only does that map show that Canadians' values are significantly different from (and more postmodern than) Americans', it also reveals that the two countries' values are actually becoming *more disparate*. As Americans have moved down and left from 1992 to 2000, Canadians have moved down and *right*.

I invite my fellow Canadians (despairing nationalists and otherwise) to forget, for a moment, split-run magazines; Amazon.ca; the long, slow death of the CFL; the imminent emigration of the Montreal Expos to Springfield, any Springfield, U.S.A.; the ominous coughing and sputtering of the Canadian publishing industry; the seeming eagle-in-beaver's-clothing Canadian Alliance; the constant hectoring by conservative newspaper columnists and right-wing economists; the *crise-du-jour* of Heritage Minister Sheila Copps. Instead, look at the story that ordinary Canadians and Americans have told us during the past decade about their own evolving values.

Trajectory of Social Change in the United States and Canada (1992–2000)

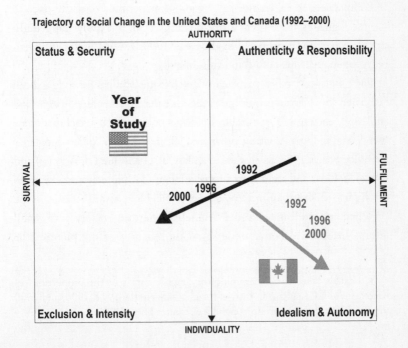

When looked at from the perspective of the proportions of Canadians and Americans dwelling in each quadrant, we see that America's Exclusion and Intensity quadrant is growing steadily, at the expense of the three other U.S. quadrants.[3] In Canada, the proportion in this quadrant remains static over the decade.

When Canada and the United States are compared in terms of the proportions of each country's population dwelling in each of the four quadrants, the differences between the two societies' social values are plain. Canadians are far better represented than Americans in the Idealism and Autonomy quadrant, and far less present in the more nihilistic Exclusion and Intensity quadrant. As for the upper reaches of the map, Canadians are overall less present than Americans, but to the extent that they reside in the upper quadrants, Canadians tend to fall on the right side of the map—the Fulfillment end of the Survival versus Fulfillment axis.

The three-point story of social change in America from 1992 to 1996 to 2000 is a story of an increasingly disconnected and disaffected society. In comparison, social change in Canada seems set on a one-way track to utopia. Canada's three-point story proceeds from a slightly more traditional, deferential worldview in the early 1990s toward increasing flexibility, openness, autonomy, and fulfillment.

For a social researcher, particularly one like me who has for so long been fascinated by Canada's quirks, virtues, neuroses, and supposedly (and endlessly) "endangered" status, it simply does not get much juicier than these two diverging lines: America's down and left into a *Blade Runner* jungle (as in Ridley Scott's 1982 classic dystopian fantasy of a future Los Angeles) and Canada's down and right into a relative Eden—or more accurately, given our high rates of urbanization—a relative New Jerusalem.

When my colleagues and I segment American society into small groups in order to better understand the nuances of the picture (the

---

3. Readers who wish to examine the graphic details of the proportions of Americans and Canadians in each of the quadrants in the 1992, 1996, and 2000 surveys are invited to consult Appendix E, figures E5 and E6.

picture of which I am of course offering only the broadest brush strokes at the moment), our results invariably include one group of extremely postmodern individuals: Americans who are open to change and diversity, who can accept and even celebrate difference not only in others but within different parts of themselves, Americans who seek fulfillment through inward exploration and contemplation, not through conspicuous displays of wealth and status. These individuals *do* exist in American society, and we find them, of course, down in the lower-right corner of the Idealism and Autonomy quadrant of the U.S. map. It is astonishing (and I imagine heartening to many readers) that when we plot the *average* position of *all* Canadians on the American map—Canadians of all races, ages, genders, incomes, levels of education, political orientations, sexual orientations, religions, regions, and so on and so on—that average falls in almost exactly the same spot as the average position of the most progressive social values segment in America. Pretty remarkable for a people who are often said to be Americans in everything but name. That there are as many as one in five Americans—that's over 55 million people—in the lower-right quadrant, which we label the Idealism and Autonomy quadrant, is not surprising, as their presence helped us define the axes of the U.S. socio-cultural map. What is surprising is that, unlike in Canada and the European countries we have studied, these people are not leading the way as some would hope or suggest, such as sociologist Paul Ray, who calls them Cultural Creatives. Nor do they espouse the "ethic of commitment" that Daniel Yankelovich had hoped would influence America's future when he wrote *New Rules* in 1981. They are one segment, or to use our term, one "social values tribe," but unlike the far fewer 15,000,000 Canadians in this quadrant, representing half their country's population, these Americans are not the defining segment in their country, nor are they the leading edge. They look more like an endangered species. But who knows—they or their successors might have another inning or two at bat before the end of the game.

Canada–U.S. Quadrant Comparisons
1992–1996–2000 Combined

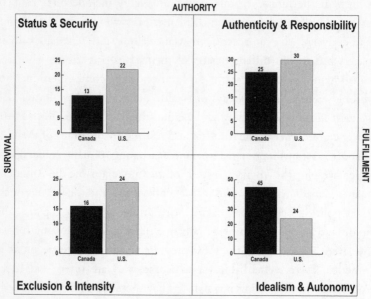

It is clear from this research that Canada and the United States are socio-culturally distinct and will remain so for many years to come—perhaps indefinitely. And whatever strange, alarming, impressive, admirable, or frightening changes may take place south of the border, Canadians will continue to behold them from a place apart. Historical, geographic, and institutional differences between the two countries have placed Canada on a separate footing—one that is not, despite the claims of many Canadian cultural critics and worriers, being eroded by winds and waves of change coming north from the American republic.

three

LOOKING WITHIN: AMERICAN DIVERSITY, CANADIAN CONSENSUS

*Where you're from [in America] is taken as a good
indicator of where you're coming from.*
—Joel Garreau, *The Nine Nations of North America*

Americans are like Canadians on speed.
—Josh Freed, columnist and author, interviewed by Peter Gzowski
on CBC Radio's *Morningside*, 15 November 1994

As a SOCIOLOGIST, weaned on the writings of Karl Marx, Max Weber, and Marshall McLuhan, I have always relished the big picture. I have spent decades accumulating tiny bits of data—21 per cent of Ontario farmers think X, 42 per cent of Maritime voters trust candidate Y—and assembling them to create stories, big pictures, that are not only empirically defensible, but that make at least some intuitive sense to other people. Social science—or "soft science" as it has been somewhat pejoratively termed by people in lab coats—poses a special challenge because, in a sense, everyone has access to at least a little data regarding the trends we report on. A biologist can walk into a room full of laypeople and say "Tse-tse flies are hermaphrodites," and not many people will demur. But if I walk into a room and say "At the beginning of the twenty-first century, Canadians are more autonomous people than Americans," a tide of challenge and dissent rises immediately.

People are especially likely to bristle at the big picture I offer (no matter how much evidence affirms it) when it doesn't correspond to what they see around them. When the Conservative Harris government won its second straight majority in Ontario in 1999, one could sit in a restaurant or walk down the street in downtown Toronto and hear more than one person exclaim, "But it doesn't make sense. I don't know a single person who voted Tory." Meanwhile, tens of thousands of suburbanites were gazing out at the blue signs on their lawns, nodding with satisfaction at the plainly intuitive outcome of the election. Of course, the aforementioned baffled Torontonians weren't *really* baffled (just frustrated): they knew that some people, even people they saw every day, had voted for the Harris Tories. Theirs is a feeling with which most of us can identify, though. Who has not read a newspaper headline at some point, one that was ostensibly about them—"Ontarians Give Harris Second Nod" or "Canadians Favour Same-Sex Unions" or "Prince Edward Islanders Eagerly Await Royal Visit"—and thought, *Not me*. And, maybe more importantly, *Not the people I know*.

The big picture, no matter how legitimate or by and large true, is almost never the whole story. This is particularly so in North America, whose population is so diverse and whose regions are so large and distinct that the big picture almost always demands some qualification. In this chapter I will discuss some of the nuances of the story I've told so far, paying attention to the differences among socio-demographic groups, asking questions about how region, age, gender, education, and income affect Canadians' and Americans' social values.

Even these more nuanced stories are themselves big pictures of sorts. Our socio-cultural portraits of American women, say, or young Canadians, or men with graduate degrees, or New Englanders are no more absolute than the portraits of Canada and the United States I am about to complicate and qualify. But the fact that these stories don't account for every shade and paradox in every population certainly does not mean that they are without value. Just as it is fascinating and instructive to find defensible generalizations about societies, it is fascinating and instructive to break societies down into component parts to see how those parts behave and how they influence the whole. Analysis of socio-demographic groups gives us access to important information, not least of which is an understanding of how certain categories (gender, age, region, etc.) cause us to differ, and, perhaps even more interesting, which categories *fail* to give rise to meaningful differences.

REGION

The day-to-day federal life of both Canada and the United States requires that those two giant national abstractions be invoked almost constantly (albeit often in unflattering terms). We all identify to greater or lesser degrees as "Canadians" or "Americans," even though we generally see only a tiny fragment of our huge sprawling countries and ever really interact with only a handful of our fellow citizens. "How Canadian," we say of friendly, hard-working Maritimers, sarcastic, laid-back Montrealers, and adventurous, outdoorsy Rocky Mountain dwellers—three very different kinds of people in very different places. Similarly, the gregarious patriarch cooking up some "barbecue" in the American South, the slick, smart movie mogul in L.A., and the jaded Jewish intellectual New Yorker all seem quintessentially American. Regional differences in Canada and, as I hope to demonstrate, especially in the United States are vast. They are also crucial to the way North Americans on different parts of the continent understand the world around them.

America's regions have experienced distinct histories and cultivated distinct cultures from the various moments settlers first set feet on their various soils. In the early nineteenth century, Tocqueville emphasized the stark differences between North and South, East and West. Walt Whitman, seeking to incorporate the entire nation into his sprawling persona in "Song of Myself," knew he had a lot of ground to cover: "At home on the hills of Vermont or in the woods of Maine, or in the Texan ranch, / Comrade of Californians, comrade of free North-Westerners (loving their big proportions) . . . ." Many of America's great writers have been embraced not for their ability to evoke the nation, but for their ability to credibly evoke some portion of it and affirm that part as at once entirely itself and entirely American: Robert Lowell's New England, William Faulkner's Deep South, and John Steinbeck's California come to mind.

Despite the fact that economic integration and new communications technologies are said to be rapidly "shrinking" the world (and with it, presumably, the United States), these regional disparities remain significant. Before 11 September infused George W. Bush's presidency with a gravity (and, some would say, a legitimacy) it had not previously known, the president returned to his home state of Texas on a "Home to the Heartland Tour," determined to show everyone back at the ranch that he was still from down home—and was holding fast against the evils of Washington, D.C.: its influence peddling, its baroque bureaucracies, its secularism, its suspiciously good grammar.

Joel Garreau, in his 1981 book *The Nine Nations of North America*, wrote, as quoted above, that in America, "'Where you're from' is taken as a good indicator of 'where you're coming from.' You can hear that in the way folk modify their answers. A person not proud of coming from Oklahoma, for instance, might add hurriedly, 'But from right down near the Texas border.' A Texan might add, 'But I went to school back east.' An administrative assistant in Washington, D.C., might hasten to stress his ties to California. But in California you'll find people who make a point of looking you right in the eye and stressing that their people came from Oklahoma. In the *Depression*. ('Want to make something of it'?)"

And Canada, as most readers of this book will know, is not without its regional loyalties either. When the regions of North America are plotted on our socio-cultural map, it is abundantly clear that Canada and the U.S. are anything but a pair of monoliths. We begin our look at the socio-demographic positioning of the continent's regions in the lower-right corner of the socio-cultural map. As I have noted more than once, this is the most postmodern quarter of the map. The Idealism and Autonomy quadrant combines an inward-looking emphasis on personal fulfillment with an enlightened individualism that rejects traditional forms of authority.

The Regions of North America on the Socio-Cultural Map

AUTHORITY

Status & Security

Authenticity & Responsibility

Region

Deep
South

Plains
Midwest

SURVIVAL

Texarkana South
Atlantic

FULFILLMENT

Saskatchewan
Atlantic
Manitoba
Alberta
Ontario

Mid- Mountain
Atlantic

Pacific New
England B.C.

Quebec

Exclusion & Intensity

Idealism & Autonomy

INDIVIDUALITY

The two regions whose residents' responses to our surveys placed them nearest this bottom-right corner of the map are British Columbia and, even more remarkably, Quebec. British Columbia's position on the map is likely intuitive to many. The province is known for its low-key attitude and way of life; people who move west from more frenetic easterly places revel in the fact that their new neighbours think more about their gardens than about their positions in some corporate hierarchy, and are more intent on mastering tricky yogic postures than on finding the most eye-catching automobile on the coast. Known as health-conscious and nature-loving, it is little wonder that denizens of Canada's West Coast find themselves on the extreme right of our map: a zone that indicates inward quests for fulfillment, which may involve anything from communing with nature to meditation to exercise—and most likely some combination of all three. A population living in a moderate climate juxtaposed between majestic mountains and a seemingly limitless ocean the rest of the nation labels Lotus Land makes a strong case for the "geography is destiny" school of social values. Is it any wonder that in its 1 March 2001 edition *The Economist's* Intelligence Unit rates Vancouver as the most livable city on the planet? British Columbians are strong on *Effort Toward Health and Spiritual Quest*. We find high levels of *Introspection and Empathy* on the coast, and also a population that believes in keeping life interesting by kicking up its heels periodically: *Importance of Spontaneity*. We also find high levels of some of those "granola" trends one would expect: *Discriminating Consumerism, Ethical Consumerism,* and *Skepticism of Advertising*.

Quebec's position is considerably more surprising. From a society with staunch Catholic roots (implying not only deference to religious and patriarchal authority, from your parish priest right up to the Pope, but hierarchy, belief in the traditional family, duty, and propriety—quite a potent cocktail of traditional values), Quebec has evolved into the most postmodern region on this continent, a status that is at least partially explained by the fact that only 29 per cent of Quebecers now believe in the Devil and fewer still, 26 per cent, believe in Hell, the lowest propor- tions, by far, of any region on the continent—the 3 per cent differential apparently made up of those who think the Devil is with us, not in the afterlife. In part this evolution from tradition to postmodernity can be attributed to intergenerational change among old Quebec families, but it also owes much to waves of immigration that have introduced to Quebec diverse thousands of "allophones" from around the world.

Quebec is exceptionally strong on bottom-of-the-map autonomy values such as *Flexible Families* and, less so, *Sexual Permissiveness*. It shares British Columbia's *Skepticism of Advertising* (all that federal government anti-separatism propaganda in the 1990s could well have had the reverse effect) and, true to its major city's reputation for hedonism, it registers high levels of *Sensualism*. Quebec's hedonism is rooted in quotidian pleasures: a glass of good wine (or two) with dinner, a lingering brunch on the weekend, meeting friends at a bar on rue St. Denis after work. The city of Montreal is renowned for its joie de vivre, café society, and active night life. It combines the tolerance of Amsterdam, the élan of Paris, and the fine dining of the San Francisco Bay Area to emerge as Canada's most sophis- ticated metropolis. Like pre-1960s Greenwich Village, Montreal's Plateau

Mont-Royal neighbourhood with its youthful, bohemian population leads the city in pleasure-seeking (although, like the erstwhile residents of New York's Village, young, cool, and poor Plateau dwellers are beginning to lose their turf as the area's rents climb out of reach and once famously cheap walkups are transformed into condos for the young executive). Hedonism in Quebec is not the brash or crude sort we find in some parts of the United States (and to a lesser extent in other parts of Canada), where *Ostentatious Consumption* and *Advertising as Stimulus* shoot off the charts.

In Quebec the more retrograde members of the sovereigntist movement may agree with former premier Jacques Parizeau that the "ethnic vote" is harming the separatist cause, but their narrow chauvinism is running against the tide: *Xenophobia* is lower in Quebec than in any other Canadian region, with the exception of the Maritimes. Just trailing Quebec and B.C. on the road to postmodernity are Ontario and the most postmodern region of the United States, New England.[1] Ontario is of course home to Canada's largest city, and it is not surprising that its many urbanites, who are used to living amid, and in many cases embracing, a diverse population (diverse in terms of race, religion, gender identity, sexual identity, economic circumstance, and domestic arrangements), would push it into the Idealism and Autonomy quadrant of the map. Ontario is also the Midwest of Canada: it falls more or less in the centre of Canada's regions on the socio-cultural map, just as the Midwest falls at the centre of America's regions.

New England has developed a reputation as one of the most (according to our data, *the* most) progressive regions in the United States. Massachusetts was the only state in the union to vote for George McGovern rather than Richard Nixon in 1972. That status has developed for a number of reasons, not least of which is that the New England states are home to more universities per capita than any other U.S. region. Academics, for reasons that are widely debated, are generally understood to be politically left-leaning, and postmodern in their values. And although professional intellectuals per se don't make up a huge proportion

---

1. See Appendix D for the composition of U.S. regions.

of New England's population, the cultures of universities (and university towns) are heavily influenced by those intellectuals. Many picturesque New England towns are home to enough vegetarian restaurants and aromatherapy candle vendors that one begins to wonder whether they can really exist in the same country as Texas or Kansas.

To the left of New England on the socio-cultural map, we find the Pacific region. Many readers might wonder at this region's distance from the Fulfillment end of the map, given the West Coast's penchant for "self work": spiritual quest, exploration of faith traditions from around the world, experimentation with exotic foods and herbal concoctions. But this stereotype applies primarily to residents of San Francisco and Northern California (and to a lesser extent those in Oregon and Washington State). Drawing the region left on our map are the conspic-uous consumers and fashion slaves of Los Angeles and the rest of the fast-cars-and-big-wallets "SoCal" area. Looking at the right-hand zone of the Exclusion and Intensity quadrant, we find trends that characterize the stereotypical Angeleno: *Sexual Permissiveness, Penchant for Risk, Joy of Consumption, Attraction to Crowds, Enthusiasm for New Technology,* and that pillar of the entertainment industry's demand curve, *Personal Escape.*

Just above Ontario on the socio-cultural map, we find Atlantic Canada and the Prairie provinces—Manitoba, Alberta, and Saskatchewan—almost on top of each other. These Canadian regions/provinces, the highest on the map (and still lower than more than half the U.S. regions), have somewhat more traditional values than Canada's other regions. They are more defer-ential to authority and more devoted to traditional institutions like church and family and codes of conduct such as duty and propriety. Their position on the map makes sense, given that the Atlantic and Prairie provinces are less urbanized than other regions in Canada; more traditional small-town values can be expected to have persisted longer in these regions, with their more venturesome inhabitants migrating to the larger cities or the United States in search of higher education and/or economic opportunity. Certainly, the Authenticity and Responsibility quadrant, which these two Canadian regions border, is the quadrant of (Canadian) small-town values: *Everyday Ethics, Social Intimacy, Civic Engagement, Social Responsibility.*

These are traditional values, but not reactionary ones such as those we tend to find in the upper-left Status and Security quadrant.

In Manitoba, Saskatchewan, and Alberta, we find above-average belief in the *Traditional Family, Traditional Gender Identity,* and *Duty*. But whereas in the United States high levels of these traditional trends tend to go hand in hand with exclusionary and discriminatory values such as *Sexism* and *Xenophobia,* in Canada's Prairie region we find no such intolerant underbelly to the belief in traditional categories of identity. Tradition *without* intolerance seems a rare combination in the world these days.

In the Atlantic provinces we find a particularly strong egalitarian bent: *Gender Parity, Heterarchy, and Rejection of Order* are all strong in this region. And contrary to Alliance leader Stephen Harper's remark about the East Coast's "defeatist" attitude, the Atlantic provinces are strong on the value *Personal Challenge*. Perhaps this is a sign that the region is emerging from its too-long history of resentful dependence on government transfers and subsidies from the rest of the country.

Near the centre of our socio-cultural map, we find three closely clustered U.S. regions: the Midwest, Mid-Atlantic, and Mountain regions. The Midwest and Mid-Atlantic are nearly on top of each other closest to the centre of the map. This is consistent with their image (particularly the Midwest's) as the stomping ground of "middle Americans." People in these regions are thought of in America (or at least described by politicians) as "regular people" who have an abundance of "common sense" and "strong values." In an early example of what we now call spin, Richard Nixon's White House always wanted to know "how it would play in Peoria"—a mid-sized town in Illinois. I'm not sure exactly what common sense and strong values are these days in America, or of who falls inside or outside the category of "regular people." It is true that the Midwest and Mid-Atlantic regions are more or less average when it comes to the range of American values (but they are far from moderate when compared with Canada's regions: they are considerably more outer-directed and status-conscious than any Canadian region, and are more deferential to authority than most). The Mountain region is slightly more outer-directed and less deferential to authority, which is consistent with, for example, the stereotype of the rugged individualists of Colorado or Montana who are happy to go from one week to the next without stepping off their sprawling ranches to see another soul.

The Plains and South Atlantic regions are not too far from "Middle America" on our positional map. They are stronger on *National Pride, Primacy of the Family,* and *Obedience to Authority* than most other regions in America, and also report relatively high levels of *Xenophobia* and *Sexism.*

Texarkana's values pull it even farther into the Wild West of our map than the Mid- and South-Atlantic regions. The region that made famous that menacing utterance "Git off my land" is strong on both *National Pride* and *Xenophobia.* And the region that includes Texas, whose state law once allowed the husband of an unfaithful woman to protect the homestead by killing his wife's paramour with impunity and where, according to the March 2003 edition of *The Atlantic Monthly,* 289 people have been executed since 1977, registers a strong belief in both *Patriarchy* and *Primacy of the Family* and the indispensable *Acceptance of Violence.* There is little in our values profile of the Texarkana region to controvert the stereotype of the ranch patriarch presiding over his family as over his cattle, guarding his own with a keen eye and a ready firearm.

The Deep South is even more survival- and tradition-oriented than Texarkana. It is the region that we find most deeply entrenched in the Status and Security quadrant of our map. There has been much rhetoric about the New South, which believers, boosters, and municipal politicians herald as a vibrant, dynamic place with trainloads of economic and cultural potential. The values profile of this region, however, indicates that the Old South has yet to dance out its last cotillion.

On a number of occasions we have asked Canadians and Americans to agree or disagree with the statement, "The father of the family must be master in his own house." As we saw in Chapter Two, the response to this aphorism is remarkably successful at differentiating Canadians and Americans on the basis of their deference (or, in the case of Canadians, their *lack* of deference) to patriarchal authority. As it turns out, this item is equally successful in differentiating the regions of North America from one another. If I were a politician or a spin doctor, I would say that this is truly a "wedge value."

The graphic below displays the vastly different responses to the "Father must be master" question in the various North American regions. Perhaps the most obvious point of interest here is the huge disparity between the most patriarchal regions (the Deep South, for example, at 71 per cent) and the most egalitarian ones (Quebec tips the other end of the scale at a mere 15 per cent agreement rate—a difference of fully fifty-six points). Montreal, Quebec, and Montgomery, Alabama, are at the opposite ends of North America's socio-cultural universe.

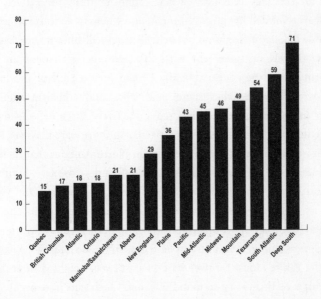

Father of Family Must be Master in His Own House
U.S. and Canadian Regions: Agree 2000

There are other noteworthy aspects of our results for this question. First is that Canada and the U.S. are completely divided—*all* American regions agree more strongly than *any* Canadian region that Father knows best. True to stereotype, the Prairies are the Canadian region most deferential to patriarchal authority, and New England is the least patriarchal area of the U.S. But even between these two regions—the sites at which

Canadian values in this area most closely match American values—the difference remains a not insignificant eight points.

Another point of interest apparent in this graphic concerns differences *within* the two countries. Between the two most disparate Canadian regions, Quebec and Alberta, there is a difference of only six points on this question. Between the two most disparate U.S. regions, New England and the Deep South, there is a difference of fully forty-two points. The span of disagreement among Americans on this basic question about family life and social organization is *seven times* that found among Canadians. This strikes me as one of the most remarkable pieces of data we have gathered in the past decade. In Canada—where regional differences are officially celebrated; where group identities are actively cultivated, even funded by the government; and where its various components not only talk about secession but actually hold nail-biter referenda on the subject—levels of agreement with this evocative statement are fairly uniform across the country. In the United States, land of the melting pot—where "United they stand" and where individualism reigns and group identities are either ignored or actively discouraged—regional differences on the basic issue of patriarchal authority are massive.

It is interesting that the two regions in North America that define the extremes of social values north of the Rio Grande—the U.S. South with its traditional hierarchical, patriarchal, chauvinistic values, and Quebec with its postmaterialist, liberal values—are also the regions that have come to have disproportionate political clout in their respective countries. Southerners (indigenous or transplanted, as in the Bushes) will have occupied the White House for twenty of the past twenty-eight years at the end of George W. Bush's first term in 2004, and Quebecers have occupied the office of prime minister for all but thirteen years since Louis St. Laurent took over from Mackenzie King in 1948, with yet another, albeit Ontario-born, Quebecer, Paul Martin, waiting impatiently in the wings. In 1980, Ronald Reagan cleverly began his successful presidential campaign in Philadelphia. Not the larger and more famous "City of Brotherly Love" and cradle of American independence in Pennsylvania, but Philadelphia, Mississippi, famous in its own right for being the site of the murder of three Civil Rights advocates in 1964. Part of the reason for the disproportionate clout of these two most extreme regions is that these regional tribes tend to stick together and vote en bloc for their own, and another part must surely be that the dominant values of the political culture in these two regions somehow distill and speak to the core values of the political cultures in their two respective nations.

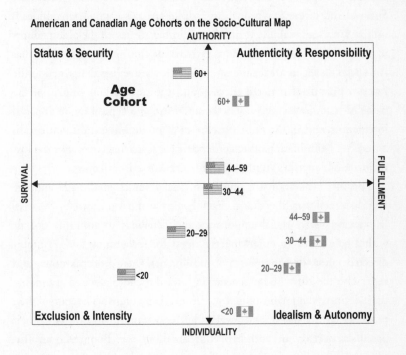

American and Canadian Age Cohorts on the Socio-Cultural Map

AGE

The placement of the two countries' various age groups on the socio-cultural map is interesting in a few ways. First, it is noteworthy that the patterns the age groups form are almost identical—a line that travels down the map from those over the age of sixty to those under the age of twenty, and arcs right and then back to the left—save that Canada's arc is below and to the right of America's arc. This means that, in any given age group, Canadians are closer to the Fulfillment end of the Survival versus Fulfillment axis and nearer the bottom-right Idealism and Autonomy corner than Americans: Canadian seniors have more postmodern values than American seniors, and Canadian youth have more postmodern values than American youth.

A second interesting point is the shape of the arc. The fact that the two youngest age cohorts in both countries, those under twenty and those between the ages of twenty and twenty-nine, have moved back toward the Survival end of the Survival versus Fulfillment axis is important. Indeed, on the American map the youngest cohort has surpassed the oldest cohort in its proximity to the leftmost extreme of the map; this means that American teenagers are leaning ever closer toward values that sanction the feverish pursuit of material success (and the ostentatious display of the fruits of that success), economic competition as a central mode of social interaction, and in the most extreme cases exclusion and discrimination as means of eliminating other contenders for scarce resources. For the vast majority of America's youth, idealism is nowhere in evidence.

The intergenerational evolution of social values in Canada and the U.S. has been roughly parallel. Each begins at the top centre of the map (a position where social conformity and deference to authority coexist with a balance of an outer-directed quest for recognition and an inner-directed quest for happiness and fulfillment), then proceeds down and right with the Baby Boom generation toward the idealism and autonomy that defined (and continues to define) that cohort. The curve then proceeds farther down, and reverses left—the youth carry on with their parents' rejection of authority, but abandon the Boomer quest for personal fulfillment in favour of more cynical and self-centred pursuits: consumption, competition, thrill-seeking.

The position of youth relative to that of their grandparents, particularly in the United States but also in Canada, is quite astounding. North Americans over sixty tend to be vastly more deferential to authority than those under twenty, and in the case of the U.S. slightly more focused on personal fulfillment (as opposed to raw survival). But while those over sixty are focused on survival, competition, and consumption within a framework of respect for authority, their grandchildren have the same (or even greater) degree of commitment to the Survival end of the spectrum—minus the respect for authority. Those over sixty have done their best to pursue the American Dream, trying to win the game of life by following the rules. Those under twenty are looking for victory—victory in the form of SUVs, expensive clothes, flashy gadgets, and outrageous experiences—but their position on the north–south axis shows that they are far less willing than their grandparents to defer to anyone's rules.

Of course, youth in Canada occupy roughly the same position relative to older Canadians as American youth occupy relative to older Americans. But when the two youth cohorts are compared, many parents if given the choice would rather have their son or daughter bring home an under-twenty Canadian than an American of the same vintage (unless they're fans of *Acceptance of Violence, Sexism,* and *Xenophobia,* in which case my colleagues and I could direct them to some gems).

When we look at the relative positions of Canadians and Americans under the age of twenty, the differences between the two groups seem less than monumental. Canadians are slightly farther down the map and fall to the right of the Americans.

But when we take a closer look at the actual values of both groups, the differences we encounter are more striking. Canadian teens, it turns out, are considerably more committed to the values we see at the Fulfillment end of the Survival versus Fulfillment spectrum, while American teens gravitate overwhelmingly to the Survival end of that axis. Here we might recall Seymour Martin Lipset's discussion of the strength of the American Dream's imperative: each generation of Americans is told, implicitly or explicitly, to succeed—or else.

This imperative may lead them to such values as *Ostentatious Consumption, Confidence in Advertising,* and *Advertising as Stimulus.* Similarly, values such as *Xenophobia, Sexism,* and *Patriarchy,* all of which are stronger for American youth than Canadian youth, may be ways of attempting both to exclude additional competitors from the harsh game of American economic life and to create static in-groups that offer some comfort and stability amid a chaotic public life. The relative attachment of American youth to *Traditional Gender Identity* and belief in the *Primacy of the Family* are also probably symptomatic of a longing for something timeless and unchanging in the face of great economic, cultural, and personal uncertainty.

Anomie and Aimlessness and *Acceptance of Violence* both reflect a society that is relentless in its pursuit of material gain: in the latter case you beat up (or shoot) the other guy, in the former you just give up and roam the streets looking for trouble at great personal risk, even of death. It's unsurprising that American youth report a greater *Fear of Violence* than Canadian youth; between their country's gun laws and the aggressive attitude of their fellow under-twenties, they have more reason to be afraid.

Canadian youth, because of the culture of relative security and stability in which they reside, are more comfortable with change and diversity. Canadians under the age of twenty are relatively more open to *Flexible Gender Identities* and *Flexible Families,* and also report a greater belief in the *Importance of Spontaneity.* They are more egalitarian in their outlook, believing more strongly than American teenagers in *Heterarchy, Gender Parity*, and *Equal Relationship with Youth*.

Canadian youth take a dim view of those peddling the trappings of the American Dream: they are stronger on *Skepticism of Advertising* than their American counterparts and are more dedicated to *Ethical Consumerism*.

They do display some remnant of their country's deferential past—call it the Collective Canadian Unconscious—in that they're stronger than their Yankee cousins on *Obedience to Authority,* but they also reveal their Boomer parents' stripes in their *Rejection of Order* and longing for *Personal Control*.

When we look at the values profiles of Canadian and American youth, two very different portraits come into focus. While Canadian youth may ultimately be travelling a path with parallels to their American counterparts, they're not only travelling that path at a much slower pace, but have started from a significantly different origin. Canadian youth *are* more "American" than their parents and grandparents, but they remain vastly *less* American than Americans. Credit the fact that while their consciousness may be overwhelmingly dominated by American popular culture, they live in Canada.

Look again at the two arcs that describe the social values of various age groups in the two countries: the arcs do *not* converge; the distance between each cohort and its counterpart in the other nation remains more or less constant, and, if anything, Canadians under the age of sixty are farther away from Americans of the same age than Canadians over the age of sixty are from *their* U.S. compeers.

This finding is not surprising, since these latter Canadians and Americans lived at a time when the values of the two countries were converging due to the common experiences of the Great Depression, the New Deal/social welfare state response to it, fighting side by side in World War II, embracing the materialism of the affluent society of the 1950s, and standing shoulder to shoulder in the Cold War. But the picture of subsequent generations is a picture of anything but convergence. Rather, it is a portrait of difference that will continue to play out for decades to come. Canadian youth watch American television, go to American movies, listen to American pop music, and wear Tommy Hilfiger's red, white, and blue. They may even admire Eminem. Nevertheless, at least as far as their Canadian distinctiveness is concerned, Canadian kids remain Canadians, and I believe they will carry that distinctiveness with them throughout their adult years and into old age—that is, well into the latter half of the twenty-first century.

Further evidence of the divergence is found in the analysis of the changing profiles of values held by Americans and Canadians in comparable age groups over the decade of the 1990s, as revealed in our surveys and presented graphically in Appendix E, figures E7 to E11. The moving picture, like that of the locomotive in the Lumière brothers' first film, is even more evocative than the static portrait I have just painted.

Over the three surveys we conducted in 1992, 1996, and 2000, Americans over the age of 60 barely moved at all on our socio-cultural map; they stayed firmly planted in the security of their traditional values of family, church, consumption, and patriotism. The only significant values found to be increasing among older Americans over the decade of the 1990s were *Saving on Principle* (now that this cohort was approaching, if not already in, retirement) and two increasingly society-wide values of *Parochialism* and *Acceptance of Violence* as a normal part of everyday life. Their relative stasis in terms of social values contrasts markedly with the evolution of other age groups in the United States over the decade.

Americans aged forty-five to fifty-nine, thirty to forty-four, and twenty to twenty-nine all moved down the socio-cultural map, departing from conformity to traditional values and norms to greater individuality and from fulfillment to ostentation and a social Darwinist mindset. Each of these age groups saw dramatic increases over the decade in a mental posture that embraced *Parochialism, Acceptance of Violence, Sexual Permissiveness,* and *Xenophobia*. This was particularly true of those aged twenty to forty-four. Each age group under sixty also scored increasingly strongly on *Sexism,* a reaction to the once politically correct feminism that was ascendant in the 1970s. They also managed to combine an increasing propensity for *Ostentatious Consumption* propped up by a growing *Confidence in Advertising* with an undoubtedly guilt-ridden penchant for *Saving on Principle*. Being in debt up to one's eyeballs tends to remind one of the wisdom of saving for a rainy day, or at least until the next sale at Wal-Mart.

These Americans could see their world becoming more competitive, but rather than retreat, they further embraced the American Dream, as evidenced by their increasing *Penchant for Risk* and *Adaptability to Complexity*. As the decade progressed, they increasingly believed that the economy would remain buoyant and that they would find a way to prosper.

American teens over this decade reflected the evolving portrait of their older peers and parents, only more so. *Acceptance of Violence, Sexual Permissiveness,* and *Xenophobia* were trends that increased among teens quite dramatically over the decade. They too were more oriented to *Ostentatious Consumption* and, as with the middle-aged, they increasingly accepted risk *(Penchant for Risk)* and increasingly felt they could adaptively navigate the often shark-infested waters of American life *(Adaptability to Complexity)*. Like their elders, they increasingly rejected the idea that boys and girls should be equal. Next to *Xenophobia, Sexism* was the most strongly increasing value among American teens in the 1990s.

Canadians, by contrast, went in another, nearly opposite direction over the last decade of the 1990s. All Canadian age groups, like their American cousins, moved down the socio-cultural map away from conformity, deference to authority, and tradition, as illustrated in figures E7 to E11 in Appendix E. What is opposite is the movement of the Canadian cohorts toward the lower-*right* Idealism and Autonomy quadrant of the map while the Americans were moving toward the lower-left Exclusion and Intensity quadrant.

Whereas the profile of American elders aged sixty and older did not change very much over the decade, their Canadian peers increasingly embraced values generally characterized with the quadrant labelled Authenticity and Responsibility. The value that grew most among Canadian seniors in the decade was *Flexible Families*, a remarkable finding since most of them had built their lives around the idea of a family being Mom, Dad, and 2.5 kids. The experience of their children and grand-children had perhaps shown them alternative definitions, which they had not chosen for themselves but decided could be accommodated in their own moral universe.

People in this group also found themselves more prone to seeing the *Importance of Spontaneity,* an indulgence they could now contemplate as they approached retirement or settled further into their hard-earned smelling-the-roses period. Consumption-related values such as *Ostentatious Consumption, Joy of Consumption,* and *Confidence in Advertising* were proclivities generally in decline for Canadian seniors during the 1990s, unlike for their American age peers. Bad news for retailers in Florida trying to pry some cash loose from those notoriously tight-fisted "snow-birds" each winter.

The contrasts between Canadians and Americans of comparable age become even more pronounced when we look at the younger cohorts. Canadians aged forty-five to fifty-nine in the 1990s could not have been more different from their Baby Boomer American cousins. The same is true of those aged thirty to forty-four and youth aged twenty to twenty-nine. Each of these age segments in Canada migrated more deeply into the Idealism and Autonomy quadrant during the 1990s, while their American counterparts made a beeline toward Exclusion and Intensity. The values that young and middle-aged Canadians increasingly embraced in the 1990s include *Flexible Families* and *Equal Relationship with Youth,* and none of the *Sexism* on the rise south of the border.

These Canadians were not as attracted as their U.S. counterparts to consumption-related values, but they did share with Americans a growing *Penchant for Risk,* combined with an increasing sense of *Personal Creativity* not found in the U.S. All these age groups saw a growth in *Parochialism,* but in Canada this growth occurred without a concomitant rise in *Xenophobia.* Moreover, a trend emerged among these Canadian age groups that was completely absent among their U.S. peers: a huge increase in the value *Spiritual Quest* as they endeavoured to fill the vacuum in their lives left by their previous retreat from conventional religious belief and practice.

It is not just among the elders, middle-aged, and twenty-somethings that we saw a radical divergence in the evolution of values in the two societies; it was also among teens, the group one would hypothesize would have the most Americanized consciousness and lifestyles, given the prodigious amount of American television, movies, music, and Internet sites to which they had been exposed all their lives. Whereas American teens profiled above moved more dramatically than any other age group into the heart of Exclusion and Intensity in the 1990s, most Canadian teens stayed firmly planted in the quadrant we label Idealism and Autonomy. Frankly, the profile of teens reveals more autonomy than idealism, although our Canadian research reveals a healthy number of idealistic "New Aquarians" among Canadian youth.

To be sure, when compared with other Canadians, Canadian teens are significantly more American than the rest of society: more oriented to consumption-related values, more attracted and inured to violence, more risk-taking, and more sexist. But when they are compared with their U.S. peers, they seem both pretty conservative and pretty liberal as opposed to anomic, alienated, violent, and excluded. Yes, they are becoming more sexist, but the values that increased most among Canadian teens during the 1990s were not *Sexism* but *Primacy of the Family, Emotional Control,* and *Skepticism of Advertising.* These kids love *The Simpsons,* but they watch the show with the appropriate degree of ironic detachment—not as a mentoring session.

Cynics might dismiss this analysis of divergence by pointing to the obvious movement down the map of each successive age group in each country, contending that each is being equally propelled by forces that cause them to abandon tradition and embrace individuality. What these cynics and disciples of convergence fail to see, in my view, is the ever-widening divergence among North Americans between an individualism that is increasingly alienated and nihilistic on the one hand and rebellious and idealistic on the other. The American version is emerging in a climate of increasing fear, chaos, and social division; the Canadian version in the context of peace and social cohesion.

GENDER

In both Canada and the U.S., men tend to reside left of and below women on the socio-cultural map.[2] This is true both of men and women overall, and of men and women in any given age group (except the sixty-plus cohort). In this oldest cohort, women actually reside closer to the Survival end of the horizontal axis and slightly below men on the Authority axis.

Of course, controversy abounds about the causes and extent of differences between men and women. Some claim that all gender differences arise through cultural conditioning, while others contend that such differences are biological or evolutionary in nature and are unlikely to ever be eliminated. Most concede that some combination of biology and social experience accounts for gendered behaviour and sensibility.

In any case, an oft-repeated observation among those who study sex and gender is that women tend to manifest a greater degree of connectedness and empathy than men do, while men tend to exhibit more individualistic and competitive inclinations. Proponents of a biological explanation for gender difference, such as David P. Barash, claim that this female propensity for attachment is the result of an evolutionary history that has rewarded males proficient at beating out other males in the quest

---

2. Readers are invited to see the graphic display of American and Canadian women on the socio-cultural map in Appendix E, Figure E12.

to inseminate numerous females, while it has favoured females who have been able to successfully nurture and foster the viability of their offspring. In this context, it is not competition but cooperation that is a winning strategy—cooperation both with other mothers and with those being cared for. Whatever the causes, women do consistently appear nearer the Fulfillment side of our socio-cultural map than men—a position that correlates with intimacy, empathy, and connectedness.

When we generate lists of men's and women's values, ranging from the values each sex espouses most strongly to those each sex renounces most emphatically, among women we find a strong affinity with *Introspection and Empathy, Primacy of the Family, Global Consciousness,* and *Search for Roots.* All these are values of connectedness; and they tend to fall near the Fulfillment end of the Survival versus Fulfillment axis. Those same values are among those we find to be weakest among men. By contrast, men's strongest values (the top five are *Patriarchy, Sexism, Acceptance of Violence, Penchant for Risk,* and *Sexual Permissiveness,* all of which are rare among women according to our data) are found much nearer the left-hand side of the horizontal axis.

As for men's and women's relative positions on the north–south axis, our map shows women in all age categories (in both countries) except the sixty-and-over cohort to be slightly more deferential to authority (slightly closer to the top of the map). This pattern may be read as something of a variation on the pattern we saw on the east–west axis. If women, for socio-historical and/or evolutionary reasons, are more inclined to "get along" (where men's inclination is to "get ahead"), it makes sense that they would be more deferential to authority than men. After all, one way of getting along is to approach others with empathy and in a spirit of care; another way of getting along is to submit to others' rules and demands.

Of course, at the beginning of the twenty-first century, few Canadians (only one in five, if we can take our "Father must be master" results as an indication) would claim that women should (or indeed do) make their way in society by submitting to men's rules and demands. Be that as it may, Canada's and America's histories (not only those that began in Western Europe, but those that are brought to North America each year by immigrants from around the world) are overwhelmingly patriarchal, and although both nations' aspirations are ostensibly egalitarian, the vestiges of our past are not erased overnight.

Our socio-cultural maps, whose portraits of men and women are remarkably consistent, indicate that, whatever we *wish* for our society, both Canadian and American men and women have been socialized in such a way that their orientation to authority, and their positions on the spectrum of inner- versus outer-directedness, are unfailingly different. Women are more deferential, men less so (except among those over sixty). Women are more outer-directed, men more inner-directed. In short, women are by and large more focused on harmony and fulfillment while men are more competitive and more focused on personal autonomy.

"You seem familiar, yet somehow strange—are you by any chance Canadian?"

But while American and Canadian women may exhibit similar values relative to the men in their societies (that is, the values differences between Canadian men and women mirror the values differences between American men and women), interesting and important differences between the two sets of women (Canadian and American) do exist. Witness, for example, the widening gap between the fertility rates of Canadian and American women. During the 1940s, 50s, and mid-60s, the fertility rate of Canadian women, that is, the average number of children produced during their child-bearing years, always slightly exceeded that of American women and reached a peak of 3.9 in the late 1950s. By the early 1970s, the rate had dropped below 2.1 in both countries, the level at which, due to an allowance for infant mortality, the population is only replacing itself, not growing, at least without immigration.

During the 1970s and 80s, the fertility rate fell well below replacement in both countries. But beginning in the 1980s and carrying through in the 1990s, the rate in the U.S. rose back up to the replacement level, whereas in Canada the fertility rate continued to plummet to a low of 1.49 children per Canadian woman in 2001. Demographically speaking, the reason is that Canadian women now postpone marriage and child-rearing longer than American women. American teenagers and women under the age of twenty-four are now twice as likely as their Canadian counterparts to have a child.

In terms of values, which are at the root of these demographic trends, the lower fertility rate in Canada almost certainly reflects the growing importance of individual autonomy in this country. Can there be a more powerful statement of personal control for a woman, at least since the wide dissemination of effective birth control and access to legal abortions, than the decision to commit to motherhood or not?

Another values-related factor in the fertility patterns in both countries is religion, specifically the relative secularism in Canada and contrasting religious observance in the United States. According to Statistics Canada, 34 per cent of American women of child-bearing age practise their religion on a weekly basis, almost double the 18 per cent found among their Canadian peers. To paraphrase the famous song, religiosity goes together with children and marriage just like a horse goes together with a whip and carriage.

INCOME AND EDUCATION

Perhaps the most significant determinants of an individual's social values, aside from the familial matrix, are the material circumstances of one's existence and the education to which one is exposed. The effects of income and education on social values can be observed on both a macro and a micro level. Ron Inglehart's World Values Survey, discussed in earlier chapters, found that as a society's affluence increases, its social values become more postmodern: diminished fear and uncertainty (due to improved financial security) bring about greater acceptance of change and diversity, as well as greater individual autonomy.

Education, of course, goes hand in hand with affluence: as a society's economic circumstances improve, citizens can begin working later in life, and retire from work earlier. Child labour in poor countries is common, whereas in Canada it is not altogether unusual to meet people in their mid-twenties who are still "finding themselves"—trying to decide whether their next move is another degree, a jaunt to Europe or Asia, or (this option is usually at the bottom of the list) a career. The period from birth to breadwinning, and thus the time available for full-time education, is compressed by poverty and expanded by affluence.

On a micro level, our data conform to the macro pattern that Inglehart observes: in general, as an individual's wealth and education increase, so too does his or her propensity for postmodern values. In both Canada and the United States, those in the lowest income brackets (who are frequently those with the lowest levels of education) reside farther up the map and farther to the left of their wealthier and better-educated compatriots. That said, the differences in values among North Americans when examined in terms of their correlation to income are not vast. Income and education do not have the final word on any individual's worldview. In general, though, it is apparent that higher levels of income and education do tend to correlate with some values, while lower levels of income and education correlate with others.

The values that tend to be most strongly affected by a person's location on the socio-economic ladder by and large fall into three related categories: control, security, and engagement. I say these categories are related because in our research we have found that the following tends to be true: people who have a greater sense of personal security (financial, emotional, familial) tend both to desire a great deal of control over their own lives and to feel they have that control. They feel their personal and professional decisions matter, and they're confident that they're able to navigate the world in all its complexity. This sense of control and comfort with complexity leads people to a greater sense of engagement with their communities and with the world around them. "I am effective in my own life," they say, "so I probably have something to offer to this community group/op-ed page/discussion/society."

Our values profiles indicate that this is the kind of worldview that wealthier, better-educated Canadians and Americans tend to hold. Obviously this is something of a caricature; no one feels perfectly in control, or entirely equal to any possible challenge. But the perspective I have just sketched shows, in a magnified way, how values associated with security, control, and engagement tend to hang together.

On the opposite end of the spectrum, *in*security tends to beget feelings of powerlessness and ultimately apathy. When people feel ongoing fear about where their next paycheque will come from, or whether their spouse is going to arrive home at the end of the day, or whether their neighbourhood is a safe place to raise kids, they begin to feel that their lives are out of their control. Their decisions don't lead to predictable outcomes, or their decisions are so severely limited by financial or other constraints that the world becomes a confusing and even a hostile place. "All right, then," some in this situation say, "if the rules can't help me, then I'm not playing this game any more." "Not playing this game" can mean anything from apathy to criminality.

Once again, this is a sketch that will probably not fit any one North American perfectly, but it is illustrative of a pattern that appears repeatedly in our findings. And the set of data I have been exploring in this book is no different. North Americans with higher levels of education and income register a stronger attachment to the values of *Personal Control* and *Civic Engagement*. North Americans with lower levels of income and education, by contrast, are stronger on *Fatalism, Anomie and Aimlessness,* and *Civic Apathy*.

four

SEPARATED AT BIRTH

One nation under Canada.
—Comedian Robin Williams

I cannot see any possible reason to annex Canada. We do not want to have
more people in the United States; what we want is to try and improve
the mob we have now. And Canada couldn't help us out. . . .
—Will Rogers, humorist popular in the 1930s, quoted in
The Best of Will Rogers (1979), compiled by Bryan B. Sterling

I'm not greatly worried by what is called the Americanization of Canada.
What people mean when they speak of Americanization has been just as lethal
to American culture as it has been to Canadian culture. It's a kind of leveling
down which I think every concerned citizen of democracy should fight,
whether he is a Canadian or an American.
—Northrop Frye, cultural and literary critic, interviewed by Robert Fulford,
"From Nationalism to Regionalism: The Maturing of Canadian Culture,"
a selection from CBC Radio's *Anthology* (1984), edited by Robert Weaver

CANADA'S HISTORY has been dominated by three great themes: building a nation and holding it together, providing a growing list of services to
the Canadian people, and managing our relations with the United States.

At the time of the American Revolution, Canada was a collection of
British colonies that remained under the protection of the British crown
rather than join the republican experiment launched by the thirteen

colonies to the south. Thanks to that revolution, we even inherited some American Tories who stood loyal to the British Empire and migrated north.

To put it in a social values context, the American colonists rejected the traditional authority of the British crown while the Canadian colonists deferred to it, or, in the case of Quebec, fashioned a pragmatic compromise between the authority the British won on the Plains of Abraham in 1759 and that of the Roman Catholic Church.

From the late eighteenth century until 1867, the northern colonies remained under British rule, although increasing numbers of colonists demanded that their governments be more responsible to them than to the colonial administrators in Britain and their agents here. Some firebrands even instigated rebellions—one in Upper Canada (Ontario) in 1837 and another in Lower Canada (Quebec) in 1837 and 1838. These were revolts against an elite of appointed officials, not revolutions against the British regime, and in neither case was there significant loss of life. Early Canadians valued a liberty based on order over a freedom derived from the chaos of mob rule, which they believed prevailed in the new republic to the south.

Whereas America was conceived in violent revolution, the Canadian colonists were counter-revolutionaries whose cautious leaders were unable to negotiate the compromises necessary for their reluctant Confederation until 1867, nearly a century after the American colonies broke from Britain. While the Canadian colonies were slowly and laboriously brokering a larger union, America was deadlocked over slavery, lurching unrelentingly toward—and ultimately embroiled in—a bloody civil war that took the lives of 620,000 soldiers representing 2 per cent of the population at that time, or nearly 6 million Americans in today's terms.

In his Declaration of Independence, Thomas Jefferson dedicated his country to the ideals of life, liberty, and the pursuit of happiness. Not to be outdone in the evocative slogan department, a century later Canada's Fathers of Confederation could see no higher pursuits than peace, order, and good government. Judged against these lofty objectives, one would have to concede that in each country "two out of three ain't bad" (Meat Loaf, 1977).

The early experience of the two countries also differed in a way that haunts America still. The southern colonies had developed an economy

Separated at Birth   105

based on slavery, an institution the United States retained (with increasing reluctance in a number of quarters) until the Civil War in the 1860s. The Canadian economy had little use for slaves or indentured workers on plantations for cotton or any other crop. As a result, the gradual abolition of slavery by Upper Canada's first governor, John Graves Simcoe, after 1793 and later by the British government was a non-issue for Canada, except to make this country a refuge for American slaves who were able to escape their servitude via the Underground Railroad prior to Abraham Lincoln's Emancipation Proclamation of 1863. The American Dilemma, as Swedish sociologist Gunnar Myrdal aptly termed that country's legacy of slavery in his 1944 book of that title, continues to express itself today—often tragically for the large proportion of African-Americans who live in poverty and under threat of violence even amid the affluence of the world's richest country.

The American Constitution also infamously guaranteed the right of its citizens to bear arms. The Second Amendment was once understood to be a provision granting militias the power to overthrow illegitimate governments through the use of force, but it has recently been recast by Attorney General John Ashcroft as the codification of the God-given right of every man, woman, and toddler to pack heat. Canada's Constitution contained no such right, and the consequences for each country are palpable to this day. Americans kill themselves and each other with the use of firearms at ten times the rate Canadians do.

America's revolutionaries, many of whom were Deists, agnostics, or even atheists, separated Church from State. Their forebears, the Puritans, had departed Britain in search of freedom to practise their religion. In founding their own communities in the New World, the Puritans were not in turn overly generous to those with dissenting theologies; Tocqueville notes that the criminal codes of some early communities included long passages copied verbatim from Leviticus and Deuteronomy. Nevertheless, 150 years later the U.S. Bill of Rights enshrined the principle of religious freedom for Puritans and all others, declaring in the First Amendment that "Congress shall make no law respecting an establishment of religion, or prohibiting the free exercise thereof."

The Canadian colonies, on the other hand, inherited the British tradition of direct state involvement in religion. After the British conquest of Quebec in 1759–60, the British not only allowed Roman Catholics to practise their religion, but, with the 1774 Quebec Act (designed to keep Quebecers loyal as the American colonies threatened open revolt), ceded to the Church the responsibility for the education of Catholic children. Meanwhile in Upper Canada, Governor John Graves Simcoe attempted to implement Anglicanism as the state religion but failed in the face of religious pluralism in the colony. The British North America Act of 1867 entrenched in Canada's Constitution the Catholic Church's control over the education of Catholics in Quebec and elsewhere in the country. This provision sought to reciprocate similar rights granted to Protestants. America's constitutional separation of Church and State and its more market-driven approach to religion has contributed to much higher rates of religious belief and practice than we now see in countries like Canada and the United Kingdom.

Another difference in the founding ideologies of the two countries was the orientation to citizenship. The American revolutionaries envisioned their country as the Biblical "City upon a Hill," a shining beacon for all who shared the Enlightenment ideals of free speech, religion, and commerce as well as progress, science, and rationality. People from all nations of the world would be welcome to cast off the chains of feudalism and migrate to the home of the brave and the land of the free. Out of many, there would be one, *E Pluribus Unum,* a proud American living in one nation, and, since the 1950s when the Pledge of Allegiance was updated, "under God." Some might argue that this ideal of unity and ultimate sameness has not been honoured from the outset, beginning with the exclusion of all but property-owning Caucasian males from the voters' list in America's first presidential election in 1789, a group that formed less than 10 per cent of the population.

In spite of many gaps between the ideal and the reality that seem obvious to us today, Americans have generally honoured their self-evident truths by welcoming migrants from around the world to join their melting pot, to become unhyphenated Americans willing to join the struggle for success and to send their sons to fight and if necessary die for their new country even against their former homelands.

Canada, by contrast, had no aspiration to mould an archetypal Canadian out of its three founding nations—French, English, and Aboriginal—or subsequent waves of newcomers from every corner of the planet. Each of the founding groups found themselves in their own enclaves. In the case of the Aboriginals, relocation was often forced and to be followed by various abuses; in the case of the French in Quebec, the enclave has always enjoyed considerable sovereignty. Sociologist John Porter characterized Canada in 1965 as a Vertical Mosaic, with the descendants of the English and the Scots at the top of the socio-economic hierarchy. According to Porter, all groups lived more or less peaceably in their communities, whatever their position in the pyramid, but had little to do with one another—a place for everyone and everyone in his or her place. In 1945 novelist Hugh MacLennan characterized English- and French-speaking Canada as Two Solitudes; this even in his native Montreal, where each comprised about half the population of what was then Canada's largest metropolis. The ethnic hierarchy of Canada today bears little resemblance to the descriptions of 1945 or even 1965, and the ideology of multiculturalism has promoted more positive attitudes toward racial and ethnic minorities north of the border than the melting pot creed has in the republic to the south.

The seeds of this compartmentalized but generally peaceful society are to be found in large part in the gradual decision by the British after their defeat of the armies of France on the Plains of Abraham in 1759 to allow 60,000 French habitants to retain their language and religion rather than attempt their assimilation into what were then very small Anglo-Saxon colonies in Canada. By the mid-nineteenth century, when the English-speaking Canadian provinces were more populous, so too, thanks to the "revenge of the cradle," was Quebec's French-speaking minority, which was able to successfully resist further calls for assimilation (most famously that of Britain's Lord Durham in 1839, who saw the absorption of the French as a solution to the "two nations" that he found "warring within the bosom of a single state"). The subsequent union of Canada East (Quebec) and Canada West (Ontario) ultimately proved unworkable. But the Confederation of those two colonies, as well as New Brunswick and Nova Scotia in 1867 and subsequently six others, has proven more lasting (although certainly not without its shaky moments).

When Quebec awoke in the 1950s from its traditional deference to the Church and Anglo-Saxon commercial hegemony, it launched a "Quiet Revolution," with the election of Jean Lesage's Liberals in 1960, to assert greater political control within its own borders. The response by the federal government was a Royal Commission on Bilingualism and Biculturalism, the latter concept soon extended to Multiculturalism when the one-third of Canadians whose ancestors had come from countries other than France and the United Kingdom demanded acknowledgement. The result was the official recognition of Canada's linguistic duality and multicultural heritage—the political birth of modern Canada—and the formal entrenchment of one of the most significant differences between Canada and the United States, one that has become more, not less, important over the past half-century. No government in the United States has ever adopted a policy of bilingualism (except the commonwealth of Puerto Rico, where English–Spanish bilingualism was imposed through military force in 1902), even though up to a third of the population in states like California, Texas, and Florida are Spanish-speaking. Nor is it conceivable that a state could negotiate separation from the other forty-nine. Canada, like the former Soviet Union, has acknowledged in its 1999 Clarity Act, three decades after then Justice Minister Pierre Trudeau liberalized the divorce laws, that a province can legally secede under certain conditions.

The United States fought a wrenching civil war in the 1860s over the issue of secession. The Pledge of Allegiance proclaims the U.S. not only as "one Nation under God" but as "indivisible." The Canadian union, by contrast, at least since the defeat of the French by the British in 1759–60, has always been contingent, negotiable, fragile, and a compromise with which no one has ever been completely satisfied. A separatist party has been elected to office in Quebec, and that province is not alone in having significant portions of its population at one time or another wishing to secede from Canada. (In fact, if the natural bounty under "the Rock" or in its offshore waters ever produces that long-awaited economic bonanza,

Newfoundland may beat its Quebec rival and be the first to jump ship.) Similarly, the relationship of ordinary Canadians to their government and to their country has been ambivalent. We are not a nation of patriots willing to die for the glory or even the integrity of our country. We are understated nationalists willing to fight for democratic values and to preserve the peace—typically in other parts of the world.

Federalism is the political institution that accommodates the centrifugal forces of Canada's regions, allocating responsibility for education and the delivery of social and health services to the provinces. In contrast, the parliamentary system that Canada inherited from the British has become hierarchical and quasi-authoritarian. Canadian governments rarely get a majority of the votes, but our first-past-the-post, single-member district electoral system usually gives the party with the most popular support across the country the majority of the seats, and a majority government can pretty well do what it wants: increase taxes, negotiate a free trade agreement with the United States, put in place a tax on goods and services, privatize Crown corporations, implement strong gun control legislation, legalize abortion, establish a national medicare program.

"Uninsured? That needn't be a problem. We can refer you to a very fine doctor in Ottawa."

Canada now spends 45 per cent of its gross domestic product on government services, which is close to the average for the countries of the European Union. The United States, by contrast, spends 35 per cent— including double the amount spent by the entire European Union on defence.

Part of the reason Canada has more activist government than in the United States is our governments' ability to act decisively within their areas of jurisdiction when they have parliamentary majorities—which is most of the time. Canada's British parliamentary system gives majority governments the power to do things that are popular, but more importantly to implement policies they believe to be necessary but unpopular— policies that may cause their defeat in the next election, but that are rarely reversed by the next government. The infamous Goods and Services Tax imposed by the Conservative government in 1990 was a major factor in its defeat in 1993, but the Liberals elected on the promise to rescind the tax recanted and were rewarded with re-election in 1997 because the voters had become inured to the new tax on consumption.

The Americans, in contrast, devised a system of government designed to balance power among the executive (president), legislature (Congress), and the judiciary so as to limit government. In times of national crisis, the president and commander-in-chief could wage war, but for the most part the government of the United States operates by consensus and compromise. It takes an extraordinary domestic crisis like the Great Depression of the 1930s or a reform-minded surge of idealism as in the 1960s for the country and its institutions to coalesce around national programs like Social Security (income support for the elderly), the 1964 Civil Rights Act, Medicare (health care for the elderly), and Medicaid (health care for the poor). Often in America (quite unlike Canada) it is the judiciary that initiates significant change, as in *Brown v. Board of Education* (1954), which desegregated schools in Topeka, Kansas, and *Roe v. Wade* (1973), which guaranteed a woman's right to abortion. Much of the rest of the time, the country seems content that politics be a game played in an opaque world of behind-the-scenes tradeoffs between politicians who are constantly running for re-election and the lobby groups who fund their campaigns. It is the political system itself as much as America's ideological inheritance that allows the National Rifle Association to influence legislators to constantly defy majority public opinion on the issue of handguns.

Canadian democracy is certainly vulnerable to the charge of elitism, even authoritarianism, but it is more democratic than the U.S. system if judged on the basis of predictable policy outcomes. Despots too can deliver predictable outcomes, of course, but with no democratic recourse. In Canada, majority governments can quickly adapt to reflect public opinion, or can dare to resist public opinion, making unpopular decisions in the hope that their judgments will prove wise over the long term—and that today's risky policy initiative will be the seed of tomorrow's public consensus (and hopefully "tomorrow" rolls around before the next election). If a government makes an unpopular decision that remains unpopular for long enough to bring about its electoral defeat, a subsequent government can always rescind the decision. The Canadian system of government, I would claim, does a better job of reflecting the considered judgment of the people and therefore keeping them engaged in the political process than does that of the United States.

Take, for example, voter turnout rates, the broadest measure of citizen engagement in any democracy. Voting tells us whether people believe it is worth being informed about public affairs and whether they believe their vote will make any difference. Canada has had consistently higher turnout rates than the United States, although Canadian rates have been declining over the past decade as Liberal party victories have been seen as inevitable and no big issues divided the electorate. Still, in the 1997 Canadian federal election, 59 per cent of Canada's voting-age population turned out to vote, whereas only 49 per cent of Americans did so in the 1996 U.S. presidential race. Moreover, political scientist Michael Martinez[1] points out that Canada does a better job than the U.S. in mobi-

---

1. Michael Martinez, "Turning Out or Tuning Out? Electoral Participation in Canada and the United States." David M. Thomas, ed., *Canada and the United States: Differences That Count*, 2nd ed., 2002.

lizing those with lower incomes. In 1997, 47 per cent of Canadians in the low-income group turned out to vote, whereas only 30 per cent of that group in the U.S. voted in 1996. It is my view that Canada's higher rates of political participation in large measure reflect the superiority of the parliamentary system over the presidential system in engaging citizens in their democratic institutions.

The United States is renowned for the direct democracy that the Progressives inspired at the turn of the twentieth century and that is given expression in the myriad plebiscites and referenda we see on state-wide ballots every two years. But these forms of democracy have not proven themselves to be superior to or more democratic than representative democracy; they overly simplify political choices (forcing yes/no binaries) and are often preceded by impenetrable preambles that are so complex voters turn off and don't vote at all. Furthermore, plebiscites and referenda tend to align majorities against minorities and invite private corporations and interest groups to spend lavishly when their self-interest is threatened. Such direct democracy looks to me more like mob rule than the considered judgment of the people that one would hope for in a democracy. American practice is a far cry from the occasional use of referenda in Canada on major constitutional issues like secession. (A notable recent exception was British Columbia's province-wide vote on how the government was to approach a range of issues pertaining to the province's First Nations.)

Canadian parties have platforms and policy positions that they usually try to implement once in office. The Mulroney Conservatives ran for re-election in 1988 on the single issue of implementing the historic free trade agreement they had negotiated with the United States. They were re-elected, albeit with only 43 per cent of the popular vote, and then proceeded to carry out one of the most important policy initiatives, certainly from a symbolic point of view, in modern Canadian history. Can there be a better case for the legitimacy and effectiveness of Canada's system of representative government than the election of 1988, an election that truly represented the future to the present? By the mid-1990s, three-quarters of Canadians told pollsters they supported North American free trade that by then included Mexico.

I remember being interviewed during the 1988 federal election campaign by PBS's Charles Krause, a correspondent for the then *MacNeil-Lehrer News Hour*. After capturing my pollster's wisdom on tape, Krause expressed his astonishment that a national debate on an issue of such moment would be decided in an election. He contrasted this process to business as usual in Washington, in which Congress members are not elected on the basis of a platform shared by members of their party, but on the basis of their bringing pork barrel goodies home to their districts. No wonder voter turnout rates in the United States have historically been one-third lower than in Canada. There is much less incentive in the U.S. to participate because there is so little relationship between an individual's vote for president, senator, or Congress member and outcomes in public policy. There are just too many vested interests to hijack elected politicians on their way to Washington. As former U.S. president Calvin Coolidge, a taciturn man nicknamed "silent Cal," once uttered, "The chief business of the American people is business," implying that public policy in America must be subservient to the operation of the free market.

Limited government is a cornerstone of America's political institutions and is tightly yoked to the country's founding ideology. The periods of activist government—at the turn of the twentieth century, in the 1930s, and in the 1960s and early 1970s—should be seen as aberrations. The neo-conservatism of the past two decades, beginning with Ronald Reagan's inauguration, should be viewed as a return to the norm. "New" Democrat Bill Clinton was least successful when he tried to be a liberal activist, as in the case of gays in the military or when pushing his wife's leftist notions of universal health insurance. He was at his zenith when, in league with "moderate" Republicans, he dismantled "welfare as we know it," the 1996 reform reducing American welfare rolls by one-third—a literal triage of America's poor. Americans have far less tolerance for state-sponsored dependence than do Canadians and Europeans, with the curious exception of the elderly, whose Social Security entitlement (kept cozy in its much ballyhooed "lock box") is a sacred cow that even the most right-wing conservative Republican dare not question.

Bill Clinton was successful because he beat the Republicans at their own game. He was able to preside over America at a time of economic boom and to leverage wedge "values" to engineer his re-election in 1996, values that neatly balanced the defence of social liberalism with fiscal prudence. Americans later forgave him his extramarital indiscretions because their culture had ventured much further into narcissistic hedonism than even Clinton had dared. In an era of the Jerry Springer "My life may be shit, but there's worse" ethos, Clinton's soap opera was a crime without victims—even his wife and daughter seemed only to grow in public esteem as their man got caught doing his own thing. His successor, Al Gore, who seemed to be running for Prime Minister of Canada (where he would have won by a landslide) rather than President of the United States, failed to touch the nerves of either American idealism or self-interested pragmatism. But one of his possible successors as a presidential candidate, Senator John Edwards of North Carolina, has far more potential. Edwards is a self-made litigator who has won huge settlements on behalf of his clients against negligent corporations, in the rich tradition of the American Dream that "you too can win the lottery" with a good lawyer working on contingency in tow. All he needs is Julia Roberts as a running mate and the next election is a slam-dunk for the Democrats.

Orientation to religion, government institutions, and founding ideology. These three factors fundamentally differentiate Canada and the United States, and this has long been the case. But these foundations have expressed themselves in the latter part of the twentieth century in some unanticipated ways. First let us look at the present realities that we or a French count might have anticipated 200 years ago. The United States has become the greatest nation on earth. It is the world's dominant economic and military power, and the leading innovator in the new information and biotechnologies. It is still the only nation on earth capable of mounting a concerted effort in exploring at the same time the human genome and the solar system. Its citizens have, on average, the highest standard of living on the planet, nearly half of the world's billionaires (242 out of 538 cited by *Forbes* in 2002) even after the dot-com/telecom implosion, and 60 per cent of its millionaires, the largest elite ever known in history.

(They are celebrated, with typical American understatement, as "masters of the universe.") And America is, after all, the nation that gave the world the gifts of jazz, baseball, and the giant, heady leap that was Neil Armstrong's moon walk. Not bad for thirteen former colonies that started from scratch little more than two centuries ago.

With these results, who can argue with their ideological commitment to rationality, science, technology, pragmatism, and the free forces of expression, religious commitment, and the marketplace? But how, ask Canadians, can a people so adept at making a living not figure out how to live? How can they allow so many of their fellow citizens to live in Third World squalor only blocks or a few kilometres from their fortress enclaves? How can so many believe they will win life's lottery when experience consistently shows that only one in a hundred will do so and only a handful will ever be an Oprah Winfrey, a Michael Jordan, a Tiger Woods, or a Bill Gates? And yet Americans themselves and millions and millions on this planet dream of the one big chance America advertises, a chance that almost anywhere else would be impossible even to fantasize.

As at the outset, America is a more competitive society than Canada. It is more innovative. It is also more violent and more racist. Americans worship money and success more than Canadians do. Americans are more willing to take risks in the hope that they might win than to insure against disaster in the fear that they might lose. Is it the relative economic and military importance of these two countries that explain the difference? Or is it the weather? Yes on both counts, plus those founding experiences, ideologies, and institutions, and the accidents of history that shape everyday life experience much more than the vaunted contemporary forces of global commerce and technology.

Certainly the growing gap in social values between our two countries during the 1990s described in this book must be at least partly attributable to America's emerging, after the collapse of the Soviet empire in 1989, as the world's only superpower, perhaps the most powerful ever to have existed on earth. This unique new status reduces America's need to forge multilateral alliances against a powerful and threatening adversary and encourages the U.S. to revert to the more aggressive unilateralism it demonstrated in its conquest of the American West and in President Monroe's nineteenth-century doctrine proclaiming America's right to control affairs in the western hemisphere, a doctrine now implicitly writ large over the entire planet. In this century, American exceptionalism becomes the *realpolitik* of globalization, something I believe will act to further differentiate the values of the United States from those of the rest of the developed world.

History is very much with us. The violence that was America is America. The moralism—good guys, bad guys, right and wrong, you're either with us or against us, establish moral superiority, wait for provocation and then blow them away—that was America remains America. In the first decade of the twenty-first century, we have an American government that now believes it can go it alone, with former allies relegated to towing the line, some enthusiastically, others resentfully. America is also the idealistic, some would say naive, dedication not just to a life that seems perfectly reasonable to all but martyrs with a cause; but to an individual liberty that often undermines the collective good and to a pursuit of happiness that often leads to the most trivial and narcissistic pursuits. The right of everyone to bear arms leads to the highest murder rate in the developed world. The pursuit of happiness leads to strange and saccharine theme parks, mindless television and movie fare, addiction, gambling, substance abuse, and even the often pathetic pursuit of salvation promised by huckster Christian evangelists—all diversions to compensate for a deep spiritual deficit. Absent the religion and civil society, the decline of which political scientist Robert Putnam has documented, one is left with a society hell-bent for nihilism.

Canada and the countries of Europe try to balance market forces with public policy, to reconcile the tendency for the rich to get richer and create an all but impenetrable elite with a social welfare state and policies to redistribute income from the haves to the have-nots. Such countries recognize individual rights but try to balance them with the rights of collectivities. These societies are more likely than Americans to realize that individuals can have too much freedom and that freedoms can be exercised irresponsibly by individuals to their own and others' detriment.

Canadians put greater value than Americans on peace, order, and good (read activist) government. This is the aspiration of a conservative people, as opposed to the eighteenth-century liberalism that appealed to the American revolutionaries.

The diseases of an all but untrammelled individualism are, of course, not without their desirable counterpoints. America is a more dynamic society than Canada, more creative, more innovative, more exciting, and more fun. According to *The Economist* (16 November 2002, p. 52), 700 of the world's 1,200 leading scientists work in the United States; these are the people we rely on to find the cure for cancer, the antidote for AIDS, and the key to Alzheimer's, and to best the long list of diseases that afflict people in every part of the planet.

Americans are wealthier than most people and are free to purchase all the things that money can buy: material possessions, symbols of status, and extravagant experiences. But the country is also a vastly more danger-ous place, not only because of its glut of guns, but because it has refused so consistently to value any common good, and has, over time, become something of a war of all against all. Its people, therefore, live more stress-ful lives, and grasp at extreme or exclusionary forms of order (often dressed up as "the way things used to be—in the good old days before [insert supposed plague here: lawlessness, godlessness, rock 'n' roll, immi-gration, television, feminism]") in an attempt to stay the chaos of social and economic life.

Some of the sites at which Canada's difference from the U.S. is most apparent are, somewhat surprisingly, our cities. In examining the size and density of the communities in which we live, we find that a counterintu-itive evolution has taken place. Canada, as any schoolchild knows, is the world's second largest country after Russia, but in terms of population contains a modest 30 million or so. The U.S. is a large country too, the world's fourth largest, but numbers roughly 280 million people.

What is astonishing is that in spite of all this vast northern space, Canadians are huddled in relatively few large urban centres, mostly a few kilometres north of the Canada–U.S. border. More than a third of Canadians live in one of three metropolitan areas: Toronto, Montreal, or

Vancouver. In contrast, America's three largest metropolitan areas, New York, Los Angeles, and Chicago, represent only 16 per cent of the United States population.

Canada is a more urban country than the United States. It is also more multicultural. Whereas 11 per cent of Americans are foreign born the figure for Canada is 18 per cent. Moreover, a large proportion of America's foreign born are from Mexico; in Canada they are drawn from virtually everywhere on the planet, with very large populations being East and South Asian.

As in the United States, first- and second-generation immigrants tend to congregate in cities where entry-level jobs, now often in the service sector, are located and where they are more likely to find support from previous waves of immigrants from their homelands.

What is fascinating about Canada's cities is their cosmopolitan livability, their relatively low rates of crime and interracial and inter-ethnic conflict. Toronto is arguably the world's most multicultural city, but has a murder rate only slightly higher than fifty years ago when it was predominantly Anglo-Saxon. The homicide rate in Metro Toronto (the core area of the city) has increased slightly from 1.4 per 100,000 in the 1959–61 period, when its population was approximately 1.5 million, to 2.2 per 100,000 in the 1999–2001 period, when its population had grown to approximately 2.6 million. Compare this with murder rates in major U.S. cities: in 1999 rates per 100,000 in New York City, Chicago, and Los Angeles were 8.9, 22.7, and 11.6 respectively. In the U.S. capital of Washington, D.C., the rate was a whopping 46.4 per 100,000, in contrast to only 0.36—three murders—in 2001 in Canada's capital of Ottawa where, thankfully in this case, nothing much ever happens. (The only U.S. city listed by the Census Bureau whose murder rate is lower than Toronto's is Honolulu.)

American filmmaker and social critic Michael Moore's documentary *Bowling for Columbine* examines in a very entertaining way America's gun culture. This exploration is relevant, given that 65 per cent of the homicides in the United States between 1987 and 1996 involved firearms. Moore contrasts the low level of arms-related deaths in Canada with the high levels in the U.S. and concludes that the reason for the difference is the Canadian social welfare state, certainly a factor, and the media-induced culture of fear in the United States. Moore states in the movie that there are as many guns in Canada as in the U.S., and admits to being a card-carrying member of the NRA, a status that enables him to conduct an unforgettable interview with Charlton Heston, the Moses of the American gun lobby.

Moore is dead wrong about gun ownership in the two countries. An international survey conducted in 1996 found 49 per cent of American households owning at least one firearm. The comparable figure for Canada was 22 per cent.[2] A more recent (April 2001) Environics survey found only 19 per cent of Canadian households with firearms. Like me, readers may be tempted to compare these percentages with the almost identical proportions of those in our 2000 social values surveys (as reported in Chapter Two) who believe that Father must be master in the home—49 per cent in the U.S. and 18 per cent in Canada.

The failure of American governments to pass effective national gun control laws is legendary on both sides of the border, although in March 1999 Los Angeles became the first American city to pass a "One Gun a Month" law, prohibiting more than one gun purchase by a single would-be slinger in a thirty-day period. Canada has its version of the NRA, but it also has a parliamentary system of government that can translate a public consensus into legislation. Spurred by the tragic events of 6 December 1989, when Marc Lepine gunned down female engineering students at the École Polytechnique in Montreal, killing fourteen, the Canadian government has enacted one of the strictest gun control and registry systems in the world.

Meanwhile in the U.S., Attorney General John Ashcroft is on record as supporting the NRA's dubious claim that the Constitution's Second Amendment protects the inalienable right of individual Americans to bear arms.

---

2. Richard Block, "Firearms in Canada and Eight Other Western Countries: Selected Findings of the 1996 International Crime (Victim) Survey," Ottawa: Department of Justice, Canadian Firearms Centre, 1997.

As for life in Canada's cities, in its largest, Toronto, where according to the 2001 census 46 per cent have mother tongues other than English, racial strife is minimal. Toronto WASPs by and large do not bemoan their minority status; they are either retreating into their increasingly irrelevant private clubs and legion halls or more often joining in and celebrating the multicultural parade. Toronto has ethnic enclaves but it does not have the ghettoes so infamous as those in New York, Chicago, and most tragically in Los Angeles. And of course, Toronto, like the rest of Canada, does not have a legacy of slavery, America's continuing dilemma. What Toronto does have is a diverse mosaic and fortunately an economy that provides jobs for newcomers. It also boasts the largest annual festival for African-Americans on this continent—Caribana, which rivals the Gay Pride pageant for spectacle and revelry. Both events have displaced the Orange and Santa Claus parades as the city's signature public celebrations.

Toronto, it turns out, is not just the world's most successful multicultural city but also home to the world's leading thinker on modern urbanism, Jane Jacobs. Jacobs, who was born in Scranton, Pennsylvania, migrated to New York City, where she keenly observed patterns of community life in Manhattan's Greenwich Village in the early 1960s and wrote the seminal *The Death and Life of Great American Cities*. Finding little audience for her perspective in her native land, Jacobs came north to Toronto in the late 1960s, together with a legion of draft dodgers, to write about cities and economies in the context of their histories and ecologies from the safe haven of her new urban village in the city's intellectual enclave known as "The Annex."

Ironically, while Americans have not embraced Jacobs's perspective on community planning, her urban village model is being adopted in a setting that is vital to America's much vaunted productivity: the workplace. As Malcolm Gladwell has pointed out in *The New Yorker*, American workers may prefer to live in sterile, homogeneous suburban neighbourhoods, but when they get to work more and more of them are finding themselves in versions of Jacobs's bustling Greenwich Village. Office planners are replicating the urban village in the workplace by deliberately juxtaposing people who would ordinarily never meet each other, such as product designers and marketers, who now find themselves bumping into each other informally, exchanging ideas, bonding, and becoming happier, more productive employees. It only makes sense that Americans—who spend more time working than any other modern people on the planet— would focus greater effort designing safe and functional workplaces while leaving neighbourhoods to fend for themselves. Once again we find Americans to be better at *making* a living than at living itself.

Canada's history of multiculturalism and the pattern of development that led to its urbanism have rendered its three great cities as models of vibrant and peaceful multicultural coexistence throughout the world.

America's cities, despite the monumental efforts to revive their urban cores undertaken by federal and state governments as well as local civic groups and philanthropic organizations, are struggling against the forces of suburbanization that have characterized American settlement patterns since Henry Ford mass-produced Model Ts. American suburbanization was once known as "white flight," with the theory that middle-class whites were fleeing the crime and racial tension of city cores (the subtext of that flight, of course, being the assumption that blacks and Hispanics were responsible for whatever ailed America's cities). Sociologist Alan Wolfe in his book *One Nation, After All* has pointed out that the "flight" has in fact been undertaken by middle-class people of all races and backgrounds—so instead of whites fleeing blacks and Hispanics, middle-class blacks, Hispanics, Asians, *and* whites have been fleeing the desperate poverty of the stranded urbanites who don't have the resources to escape the wasted *Blade Runner* jungles their inner-city neighbourhoods have become. As middle-class people flee America's cities, they may well relocate to more or less ethnically homogeneous suburbs and exurbs, but the real social chasm lies not between the black suburb and the white, but between the haves who drive their SUVs to relative safety outside the city and the have-nots who stay behind.

A good slice of the American Dream for those who flee the cities is a two- or three-car garage with a house attached located in a leafy suburb, now more likely a gated community with homogeneous populations (despite the multi-ethnic flight from cities, there is much evidence that the suburbs and exurbs in which former city dwellers end up are starkly segregated along racial lines) attending weekly church services with even more homogeneous congregations.

America's much vaunted religiosity, expressed in more than four in ten attending weekly church services (twice the proportion found in Canada), may have more to do with the quest for a safe refuge in a community of kindred spirits than communion with God. Even in the South, guns must be checked at the door before the entering the House of the Lord. With one in six Americans now living in gated or privately secured condominium communities located far from downtown or even residents' place of work, their American Dream community is looking more like a medieval fortress than the New England town that Norman Rockwell depicted on the covers of *The Saturday Evening Post* and that Bing Crosby, Danny Kaye, Rosemary Clooney, and Vera-Ellen take the train to each White Christmas.

Unlike Canadians, Americans are increasingly isolated from the poor, from immigrants, from the "other." This is both caused by and exacerbates Americans' fear of strangers and in turn their sense of estrangement from the larger society. Like America's gun culture, this is a vicious cycle, and it reached a tipping point beyond remediation decades ago. Americans have long seemed condemned to their flight from cities to suburbs, from suburbs to exurbs and edge cities, and now to soon-to-be-overpopulated mountain or desert wildernesses. (Ted Turner is reported to have purchased Montana so that he can be alone in his dyspeptic retirement.)

Americans pursue heaven on earth by fleeing their cities in search of bucolic bliss. Canadians, on the other hand, prefer to congregate in their cities, albeit with frequent escapes to cottages, cabins, chalets, and in winter the beaches of Florida. Canada's cities, Americans and most Canadians would be surprised to find, actually enjoy lower violent crime rates than do its small towns and rural areas.

It is interesting indeed that these two New World nations have each won the sweepstakes in two international competitions: the Americans for the highest standard of living on the planet and the Canadians for the best quality of life. The Americans have done this by being motivated by the notion of individual achievement; the Canadians by balancing individual autonomy with a sense of collective responsibility. We are each twenty-first-century expressions of the ideas of our ancestors and the institutions they built. America honours traditionally masculine qualities; Canada honours qualities that are more traditionally feminine. America honours the lone warrior fighting for truth and justice, the father who is master of his lonely house on the prairie, and a few good men planting the Stars and Stripes on a distant planet. Canada honours compromise, harmony, and equality. Americans go where no man has gone before; Canadians follow hoping to make that new place livable.

If American historian Samuel P. Huntington is right, the twenty-first century will be an often violent clash of civilizations. In that event, we will all be grateful for American economic and military leadership. If, however, the challenges of the twenty-first century will be addressing the growing disparities between rich and poor and the degradation of the earth's ecology, then let us hope Canada and kindred nations can muster the courage to show us another path into the future.

As I have demonstrated in this book, the founding ideas and institutions of each country have given rise to unanticipated consequences. I have found Americans to be more deferential to institutions than Canadians. This is counterintuitive. I have found Canadians to be less anomic, aimless, and alienated from their society than are Americans, who are nominally a more religious people. This too is counterintuitive. And, perhaps most surprising, I have found Canadians to be a more autonomous people than Americans, less outer-directed and less conformist. This too is contrary to the stereotype of Americans as a nation of individualists.

The key to these apparent anomalies, I believe, is the consequence of America's single-minded pursuit of individual achievement in the absence of peace, order, and good government. By adolescence and often earlier in life, Americans find themselves in an intense, often dangerous struggle for survival—or a winner-take-all quest for success. In such a context, traditional authorities serve as anchors: a strong father, a strong police force, a strong military, a strong nation, the president and commander-in-chief.

In such a world there is little tolerance for subtlety, nuance, or shades of grey. Life is a Manichean struggle between good and evil, winners and losers, and the only way good will prevail is by being the strongest, vanquishing the "evil empire" or the "axis of evil" or the next incarnation of the forces of evil. Bruce Springsteen, American icon and perpetual valedictorian of the school of hard knocks, summed it up in his aptly named tune "Atlantic City": "Down here it's just winners and losers—and don't get caught on the wrong side of that line." In this world, individuals must choose their side, fall into line, and follow their leader into battle. There is little room for individual autonomy in such a scenario.

Canadians, however, have found themselves throughout their history to be in an interdependent world. After the Conquest of the French by the British army on the Plains of Abraham in 1759, it was decided by the authorities not to vanquish or assimilate the Quebec colonists but to accommodate their collective aspirations to preserve their religion, language, and culture. In the nineteenth century when America suffered a bloody civil war over slavery, Canada experienced a few rebellions, but in the end negotiated compromises that eventually led to Confederation in 1867. Good never triumphed over evil in Canada. Rather, opposing forces, often more than two, fighting over geography, religion, language, or the spoils of power, eventually came to some sort of accommodation— usually with little loss of life, especially when compared with the U.S. Civil War and the near annihilation of Aboriginals as Americans settled the West.

Our founding ideas, our institutions, and then the experience of building our two nations have been very different: one by conquest, the other by compromise. This Canadian penchant for going halfway rather than fighting it out to see who's left standing expressed itself in the twentieth century with the recognition that Canada was not only bilingual but also multicultural. And now, with the establishment of the new northern jurisdiction of Nunavut (one of whose official languages is Inuktitut), Canada is formally recognizing multilingualism as well.

This penchant for compromise, I would contend, has been expressed in less dramatic but equally important ways in the everyday life of

Canadians. Feminism in Canada has become much more normative and has generated much less opposition than in the United States, as our social values data have demonstrated. The equality of women is not viewed as a threat to men or to the family, to corporate hierarchy or the well-being of the nation, as it is so often in the United States.

Similarly, when homosexuals asserted their rights, they found Canadians to be far more accommodating than the people of the United States. Montreal is a gay tourism mecca, and Toronto's Gay Pride Week is among the top three in the world in terms of attendance, having drawn an estimated 1,000,000 spectators and participants in 2002—not to mention $76 million in tourist dollars (*Broadcast News,* 27 September 2002).

The point is that the "conservative" society that values "peace, order, and good government" is also the society whose people feel secure enough to acknowledge interdependence. To be interdependent means to acknowledge the essential equality of the "other." When everyone feels equal and respected, they feel they can be in control of their own destiny in a world that relies upon the enlightened self-interest rather than the subservience of others. People in such a context have the self-confidence to be autonomous. In Canada, interdependence, autonomy, and diversity work in concert.

In functional families autonomy is cultivated by treating children with respect from day one, treating them, within reason, as equals. As in the nation, the domestic realm of the family can be governed by the ideals of peace, order, and good government with an absolute minimum of violence. Along with automatic deference to patriarchal authority, Canadians have by and large abandoned the age-old shibboleths "Children should not speak until spoken to" and "Spare the rod, spoil the child." Americans are still divided on the fundamental issues of what it is to be a father, a mother, or a child. In America, a father whose son comes out of the closet and declares his homosexuality is more likely to say, "You are no longer my son." In Canada such a father is more likely to find a way to adapt.

Thus, in Canada, the culture of accommodation that has been our socio-historical tradition expresses itself today as social liberalism, multiculturalism, multilingualism, multiple faiths and spiritual paths, and sometimes even as cultural fusion or hybridization. In its most postmodern form, it can exist as an openness to flexible, multiple expressions of individual personality, the leading edges of which are the flexibility of gender, age, and cultural identities. Demography as destiny is the vestige of a bygone era.

It is fascinating to see a country evolve from such deep deference to hierarchical authority to such widespread autonomy and questioning of authority—yet in the process not descending into chaos. Canadians are no longer motivated by duty, guilt, noblesse oblige, or fear of social sanction if they do not conform to group norms. Their kinder, gentler balance of freedom and equality, and of the public and the private domains, has created a tolerant, egalitarian society that enjoys freedom from potential catastrophe, danger, and violence that many on this planet envy, including many Americans.

But I don't for a moment think that most Americans believe Canada is a model to emulate. They are too focused on their own lives in a very different culture with very different institutions; their perspective on the global picture and their apparent trajectory of development are vastly different from our own. Canadians have always been congenitally introspective, perhaps because we have always felt threatened by internal cleavages. Americans, more preoccupied by conquest, are less introspective, particularly now that their dreams of global mastery are threatened by terrorism. Few Americans think they have anything to learn from Canada or Canadians, although plenty think they have lessons to teach us about the "real" world.

In my nightmares, I may see the American fire melting the Canadian ice and then dream of the waters created by the melting ice drowning the fire, but this will not happen—at least not in our lifetimes. The two cultures will continue side by side, converging their economies, technologies, and now their security and defence policies, but they will continue to diverge in ways that most people in each country, I believe, will continue to celebrate.

five

CLOUDS ON THE CANADIAN HORIZON

As Canadian as possible under the circumstances.
—Winning response to a *This Country in the Morning* contest that
asked listeners to "define the Canadian identity in a single, short sentence"

*Well, it's still a good place to live, but that's all
Canada is now—just a good place to live.*
—Donald G. Creighton, historian, observation made in 1979, the year of
his death, to the cultural journalist Charles Taylor, *Radical Tories,* 1992

A passion for Canada requires a delicate suspension of disbelief.
—Bryan Johnson in *Maclean's* magazine, 25 November 2002

IN MONTREAL'S OLD PORT, there is a large building containing many
strange apparatuses—massive hoops and wheels, irregular bicycles,
pulleys and hooks, kilometres and kilometres of rope. The building also
contains hundreds of exceptionally lithe and talented young people. I am
describing, of course, Canada's world-famous École Nationale de Cirque
(the National Circus School). But if you're Canadian, you've likely never
heard of it.

Founded in 1981 and offering instruction only in French, the École
Nationale de Cirque is one of the most respected institutions of its kind
anywhere in the world. Every year, it attracts would-be circus performers
between the ages of twenty and thirty from around the globe. Ask those

young people what attracted them to the school, and they will cite the quality of its instruction (students hailing from Europe offer special praise for the school's zeal for innovation; it seems some of them find the Old World's circus "establishment" stultifying); they will also emphasize the exciting international atmosphere offered both by the école and by the vital city that surrounds it. And after all, if you're hoping for a future in the circus—the highly creative, sophisticated, balletic kind of circus that has emerged as a new art form during the past couple of decades—then Canada is arguably the best country on the planet from which to launch your career.

It is hard to imagine a more apt metaphor for the postmodern side of Canada's personality than the École Nationale de Cirque. It's international. It's youthful, vital, and innovative. It's at the leading edge of exciting artistic movements. And for anyone who has seen its graduates perform in the Cirque du Soleil, it speaks a language that is universal. It's at once quirky, offbeat, and extremely graceful. And for all these things it is famous—everywhere but here.

When I wrote *Sex in the Snow* in 1997, I was eager to tell Canadians about the direction and impressive pace of social change in this country. A pronounced and exciting evolution had unfolded over the previous half-century, a half-century of remarkable technological and socio-political developments. Not only did I think Canadians would be intrigued, as I was, by the segments or "social values tribes" we had found amid the population; I thought they would also be fascinated by the vision of the future that seemed to come into focus in the values of our most postmodern youth tribes: the thoughtful and idealistic New Aquarians, the smart and resourceful Autonomous Postmaterialists, and even the fun-loving, experience-seeking Social Hedonists. The École Nationale de Cirque is just one colourful manifestation of the Canada that our data suggested was beginning to take shape at the end of the last millennium.

The story I have told so far in this book is one of a Canada that seems, when compared with the United States, a natural home for a national circus school, not to mention the government-funded Just for Laughs Museum, also located in Montreal.

In this chapter I describe the trajectory of social change in Canada, not in comparison with the United States, as I have done to this point, but solely in terms of its own culture—as I did for the United States in Chapter One.

Readers of *Sex in the Snow* and my second book, *Better Happy Than Rich?* will know that Canada has its own unique socio-cultural map. The Canadian map has parallels to the U.S. map: the north–south axis defines the movement from traditional Authority at the top to Individuality at the bottom of the map. However, the east–west axis of the Canadian map is considerably different from that of the U.S. map: it does not range from Survival (left) to Fulfillment (right) as in the U.S., but rather from outer direction to inner direction. The outer-directed are status-conscious people very much concerned with the opinion of others—wishing, for example, to gain their approval for the things they own and the symbolically evocative experiences (that trek to Katmandu) they've had while at the same time avoiding disapproval for the views they express. The inner-directed do not care what others think of the views they express, the political party they support, or the clothes they choose to wear. They march to the beat of their own drummer. Readers who are interested in a description of the macro mental postures in each of the Canadian map's four quadrants will find the details in Appendix F. Others who have found getting their heads around the American socio-cultural map challenging enough are encouraged to continue with my story in this chapter.

The sanguine analysis of Canadian society portrayed so far in this book must be qualified somewhat when we take a closer look at the recent trajectory of social change in this country.

As we saw in the description of the American socio-cultural map in Chapter One, the values at the top of our map are by and large more traditional than those at the bottom. The deference to authority at the top of the Canadian map is not as pronounced as it is at the top of the American map (which in itself should raise a few eyebrows, given the two countries' respective histories and supposed characters). Nevertheless, it is in the upper regions of the Canadian map that we find the trends that indicate confidence in and deference to large institutions, and belief in the significance of traditional markers of status and identity. The upper portion of the map also includes a certain fearfulness of change, evidenced by trends such as *Technology Anxiety* and *Aversion to Complexity*.

Given this more traditional attitude in the upper regions of the map, it is not surprising that Canadians in our "Elder" or "Pre-Boomer" age cohort (those born prior to the mid-1940s) have generally held values that have placed them in the top third of the map. Margaret Atwood has written that "the twentieth century has not been a raving success," and those in our Elder cohort have lived through the brunt of the century's disasters. These Canadians were born and came of age in a world full of insecurity and turmoil. They or their parents experienced (from various vantage points) two World Wars, the latter of which introduced into global consciousness both the horror of genocide against Jews in Europe and the spectre of atomic annihilation in Japan. They felt the effects of the Great Depression, either directly or through widespread residual fear and insecurity. They have seen religion transformed from the embodiment of humankind's highest ideals and the glue that bound communities together to the rationale for prejudice, hatred, and war. And while generally on the positive side of the ledger, they experienced technological change that transfigured the world with staggering speed: the telephone, the automobile, radio, television, electric-powered household appliances, and the airplane all came into mainstream use. These Canadians also witnessed the way these new wonders radically transformed many of the traditional patterns in their lives that they had greatly valued.

It is hardly surprising that in the midst of this tumult, the vast majority of those in our Elder cohort clung steadfastly to the values that had seen their parents through difficult times: religiosity, deference to authority, delayed gratification, adherence to strict gender roles and family structures, and a general orientation to order in personal and social life. It is noteworthy that these values are not universal in the Elder cohort: in *Sex in the Snow* I describe a fascinating segment of the Elders—a segment comprising a full fifth of that generation—whose values reveal a remarkably modern and forward-looking mental posture. These "Cosmopolitan

Modernists," as we call them, have a global outlook, an openness to complexity and diversity, and a desire for autonomy that belies their early life experience. Despite the interesting exception of the Cosmopolitan Modernists, however, in 2001 a traditional mindset still characterized those over sixty.

From the time we began performing our social values surveys in 1983 until the mid-1990s, we saw Canadians' values modernizing. Although on the whole the Elders remained traditional, the Boomer generation was leading Canadian society at large toward values of greater autonomy, flexibility, and openness to diversity and change. As I have mentioned before, social change tends to be primarily intergenerational. Therefore, Canadian society's evolution indicates that as older Canadians with more traditional values leave our sample (through temporary migration to Florida or permanent relocation to the random sample in the sky) they are being replaced by new Canadians (mostly those becoming eligible to participate in our surveys by turning fifteen) whose values are more modern, liberal, and egalitarian.

The Boomer generation, made up of Canadians born during those famously fecund years between the end of World War II and the mid-1960s, grew up in the midst of a historical period vastly different from the one that had shaped their parents' values. Postwar prosperity and the culture of optimism that accompanied it gave young Boomers the sense that basic survival could be taken for granted—an assumption in which their parents had not been able to indulge. Freed from care regarding physical security and daily survival, the Boomers had the opportunity to turn their attention to quality-of-life issues. Stirred in part by empathy with the civil rights and anti–Vietnam War movements south of the border, and influenced by cultural material from the Beat poetry of the 50s to protest, folk, and rock 'n' roll music, Canadian Boomers developed a deep streak of idealism. More quietly than their American counterparts (but, it is now becoming clear, more enduringly), these young Canadians began to advance an agenda of gender and racial equality, pluralism, environmentalism, and social justice. They never for a moment thought they would be forced or even asked to fight a war somewhere. In 1968, many of the early Baby Boomers exercised their franchise for the first time and helped elect Pierre Trudeau, who had evaded service in World War II, twenty-four years before Americans could elect as their president a man who, in his day, had managed a lateral arabesque to Oxford University to avoid fighting in Vietnam.

The Boomers' values emerged and solidified in concert with their politics. They believed that men and women were equal, and began to question not only the patriarchs within their own families, but also the branches of organized religion that prescribed those domestic gender hierarchies. They believed that people of different races and cultural backgrounds were equal, and so developed a cosmopolitan outlook, championing human rights worldwide and exploring spiritual traditions from around the globe. Having questioned if not rejected the religious institutional authority to which their parents had submitted, the Boomers also came to reject the idea of deferred gratification. Why live a life of self-denial, they reasoned, in anticipation of an afterlife whose existence is chancy at best? Why wait for retirement at sixty-five to begin to have fun only to drop dead one or two years later? Why not live life as pleasurably and ethically as possible, for as *long* as possible, smelling the roses from time to time along the way? And while we're at it, why not take care of this planet, which might just have to last our progeny a lot longer than those awaiting the arrival of the New Jerusalem might think?

As with the Elders, not all Boomers are the same. Our analysis has found, in addition to the defining segment of the cohort (the "Autonomous Rebels"), other Boomer segments that either adhere to more traditional, Elder-like values, or lean more toward feverish consumption than measured idealism. The Autonomous Rebels, however, with their individualistic, inward-looking, and idealistic values, have embodied what our society has come to understand as the Boomer ethos. Whether you consider the people I've just described to be forward-thinking cultural revolutionaries or spoiled narcissists, chances are you recognize them. And it is not for nothing that these Autonomous Rebels, the Uber-Boomers, have become culturally resonant figures. Our data show that on the whole, Canadian society until the mid-1990s was following the very path set out by these enlightened hedonists: the general movement of Canada's values directly toward the Autonomous Rebels' position in the Canadian quadrant we label Autonomy and Well-Being.

The move was dramatic. In 1983, only a quarter of the Canadian population espoused values that placed them in the most modern third of the socio-cultural map; 75 per cent of Canadians were still sufficiently deferential to authority to reside in the map's more traditional regions. By 1996, an additional fifth of the population had moved into the most modern third of the map: that meant 44 per cent of all Canadians had reached the most autonomous zone in our mapspace.[1]

The Boomers' children, too, seemed to have taken up their parents' flag of autonomy. For want of a better label, we refer to the post-Boomer cohort (anyone born after 1965) simply as Youth. With this generation, more than with either of the other two I have described, it is nearly impossible to generalize. When my colleagues and I were analyzing the data that produced *Sex in the Snow*, the Elder cohort was made up of three segments we call "tribes," the Boomer cohort of four, and the Youth cohort of five distinct groups with unique and coherent social values profiles. Three years later, when studying the data for my second book, *Better Happy Than Rich?* we found that yet another segment had emerged in our youngest age group, bringing the total number of discrete social values tribes in that cohort to six.

It makes sense that social values should become more diverse as we shift our attention to younger Canadians. As media have proliferated and communications technology and transportation have improved, and as more and more young people have obtained college and university educations, demographic characteristics such as region, age, race, and class have become much less powerful factors in the construction of young people's identities and perspectives on the world. Of course, older Canadians also have access to these innovations, but their impact on younger Canadians' values has been more profound, if only because younger Canadians encountered them at an earlier age and are now more likely to take them

---

1. This graphic detail is presented in Appendix F, Figure F6, page 200.

for granted. Because young Canadians have had, in a sense, a wider and more accessible world from which to pluck ideas and associations, their social values have become more diverse than those of their parents or grandparents.

The culture of relative freedom established by the Boomers also contributed to the diversity we see in this generation. The Boomers broke down a lot of walls in their journey from deference to defiance, and their children have by and large taken advantage of the new territory that has opened up to them. Young Canadians can make choices today that only a few decades ago would have resulted in vigorous and protracted head-shaking from family and community, if not outright rejection. Think of the relative ease with which twenty-somethings can now cohabit before marriage (if they plan to marry at all), have interracial or interfaith relationships, explore spiritual traditions from around the world, be openly gay or lesbian, or choose unconventional career paths. Of course, most of these choices will still involve some social and familial resistance, but there is no doubt that the difference between attempting them today and attempting them forty years ago is vast.

Think of the evolving role and status of women in Canada. Grandmother in the elder generation was more likely to be a stay-at-home wife and mother, and if she worked outside the home it was likely to be as a nurse (only men trained for medicine). Early Boomer women were much more likely to work outside the home than their mothers, and became teachers and social workers, playing best actress in a supporting role to husbands who had higher status and more remunerative prospects. Boomer women who came of age in the 1970s and early 80s realized the dreams of the early feminists by invading traditional male bastions in very large numbers: law, medicine, business administration, even engineering. By the time post-Boomer women came of age in the late 80s and 90s, women were actually beginning to outnumber and outperform men in the professional schools that would prepare them for the high-status occupations in the new millennium.

Two of the Canadian youth tribes we found to be most comfortable with and most successful at handling the freedoms available to them in

1996 were the New Aquarians and Autonomous Postmaterialists.[2] These two tribes were (and remain) at the cutting edge in postmodern social values. The New Aquarians were the idealists who carried the torch of equality and social justice. Just as their Autonomous Rebel forebears had fought for equality for women and racial and religious minorities, the New Aquarians were dedicated to those causes as well as new ones: ensuring that the forward march of globalization didn't trample the poor, seeking equality for gays and lesbians, and taking up compelling causes in all corners of the world using the Internet as a tool for activism and interpersonal connection. The Autonomous Postmaterialists were equally unafraid to rock the boat, but tended to do so in the world of business. They were an innovative and enterprising group, and if they were less dedicated than the New Aquarians to changing the world, they were every bit as broad-minded and adventurous in their approach to it. Both groups were extremely autonomous, flexible, and adaptable; the New Aquarians were more socially engaged, while the Autonomous Postmaterialists had a stronger individualist and entrepreneurial bent.

Six years ago, it seemed that these two most postmodern segments of our sample would lead the way for the rest of Canadian society. Values would remain diverse, but by and large Canadians would move into postmodernity, becoming increasingly confident in their ability to adapt to change, adopting an open and flexible approach to the world around them, desiring personal autonomy and freedom from authoritarian and hierarchical power structures, whether at home or at work, in civic or religious life. Just as society had to that point been following in the wake of the wayfaring Autonomous Rebel Boomers, it seemed it would follow the New Aquarians and Autonomous Postmaterialists into a postmodern future.

It struck me as remarkable, at the time I wrote *Sex in the Snow*, that these two leading segments should have emerged in Canada: the New

---

2. Canada's social values tribes are described in detail in my two previous books, *Sex in the Snow* and *Better Happy Than Rich?* Readers who wish to find their own tribe are invited to visit the Environics Web site at www.environics.net.

Aquarian revolutionaries and the individualist, freedom-loving Autonomous Postmaterialists. Weren't revolution and individualism America's bag, while we Canadians stuck to compromise, accommodation, and cooperation? The climate of relative security and stability in which young Canadians were coming of age inspired many of them to embrace values more liberal, tolerant, and adaptable than their Baby Boomer parents. In America, by contrast, we were beginning to see many young people drowning in their freedom—living in a chaotic society and responding either by grasping at rigid power structures and exclusionary group identities or by succumbing completely to the jungle mentality and renouncing order altogether in favour of brutal, even violent individualism and competition.

But the data we collected in the years following the publication of *Sex in the Snow* have shown an interesting reversal. The two ultra-postmodern "tribes" I have just described did not turn out to be harbingers of what was to come in the years following 1996. Rather than being the standard-bearers in a steady Canadian march to postmodernity, the more idealistic New Aquarians became outliers (along with the Autonomous Rebels), while the Autonomous Postmaterialists joined other Canadians, *especially* the youth, in returning to a more traditional mindset and, for some, into the extremes of Conformity and Exclusion. Thus, in the past several years, we have seen the postmodern tribes at the bottom of the map become not the leaders but the resisters of social change, since social change in Canada is at present a story of regression—a retreat to the safer and more stable space (for those who "fit in") away from flexibility and openness.

In the mid-1990s, Canadians (surprisingly, especially young Canadians) began moving backward on many fronts: from Idealism and *Adaptability to Complexity* toward conformity, exclusion, and a Darwinian perspective on life's prospects. At the same time, we observed a continuing movement away from outer direction, duty, tradition, and morality toward inner direction and hedonism. In other words, we were seeing a retreat to a more traditional mindset absent the focus on the traditional institutions of family, religion, and community. In this space, we find Aimless Dependent youth who cannot find meaning in their lives as well as a new youth tribe, the Security-seeking Ascetics, who have recently found a raison d'être and are doing all they can not to end up as one of life's losers.[3]

This reversal in the trajectory of Canadian social change was surprising, and even a little alarming. It seemed that Canadians, even our youngest, who, the story goes, are supposed to lead us forward toward more progressive, postmodern values, were abandoning the process of postmodernization in favour of more traditional (some might even say retrograde) territory that our society had already trodden generations ago. But this move back up the map should not be interpreted as a return by young people to the values of their grandparents. They are not flocking back to the churches nor clamouring to join the military. They do strive for order and stability and some are even finding it in a good job and marriage, while many others remain aimless and alienated, roaming from job to job in the low-end service economy, moving out and then back into their parents' homes like yo-yos, unable to obtain one of those more stable manufacturing or resource industry jobs that had seen their fathers and grandfathers through their early adult years. Quite simply, order and stability are perceived differently by young people today than by their grandparents.

Now, comparing the values of youth in Canada across the border rather than across time, we must ask whether Canadian youths' move up the map was a sign of Canadians moving into the American battleground: reactionary traditionalists versus directionless nihilists? What we saw in Chapters Two and Three is that the reversal in Canadian values becomes almost invisible when viewed in the larger North American context. I do not mean to imply that the change is meaningless within Canada; indeed I think it is fascinating and important. But I am convinced that the movement of the Canadian youth back up the Canadian map to a more traditional mindset offers little or no evidence of Canadian and American socio-cultural convergence.

Canadians remain distinct from their neighbours to the south, and there is no indication that the socio-cultural differences between the

---

3. This graphic detail is presented in Appendix F, Figure F7, page 201.

two nations are being eroded. For every step Canadian youth may seem to be taking in the direction of American youth, American youth take several more, travelling farther and faster along the path to nihilism and anomie. As we saw in Chapter Three, when examined in the North American context, Canadian youth are as Canadian as ever—even becoming more so.

six

THE MYTH OF INEVITABILITY

*Two nations have evolved that are utterly alike in almost all of their externals and
yet are utterly unalike in their political cultures so that they are as distinct from
each other as are the Germans from the French, say, even though both are
Europeans just as Canadians and Americans are both North Americans.*
—Richard Gwyn, *The 49th Paradox: Canada in North America*, 1985

*Americans have great and noble principles and they go to hell trying to live
up to them. Canadians also have great and noble principles but they
go to heaven figuring out ways to get around them.*
—Attributed to linguist Noam Chomsky by Christopher Dafoe
in *The Globe and Mail*, 13 March 1993

*We have become a people who, without a trace of irony,
love to yell about how modest we are.*
—Matthew Mendelsohn, quoted in *Maclean's* magazine, 25 November 2002

T HE GREAT PHYSICIST Werner Karl Heisenberg once wrote, "What
we observe is not nature itself, but nature exposed to our method of questioning." What the father of the uncertainty principle admits for the
"hard science" of physics is more than applicable to the "soft science" of
social research that informs this book and the observations and conclusions I have reached about the two cultures under investigation. To extend
the analogy, we, like the astronomer who relies upon his telescope to

fathom the heavenly bodies of our universe, put our faith in the lens of survey research to tell us truths about societies and cultures. That lens we hope is a prism revealing the many colours, shades, and hues of these two multifaceted and changing countries. Through in-depth, one-on-one interviews, focus groups, and surveys of samples we hope are reasonably representative of the entire population, we try to find out what values guide people's everyday decisions and ultimately give meaning to their lives.

Our samplings in a great civilization (America) and its mysterious neighbour (Canada) over the past decade lead us to conclude that the two countries that share so much are in fact headed in two significantly different trajectories in terms of the basic socio-cultural values that motivate their populations. This story is counterintuitive. Most people will find it hard to believe, given that Canada is increasingly dependent on the U.S. economy and that Canadians consume increasing amounts of American popular culture, products, services, and imagination.

In Chapter Four I tried to explain why Canadians and Americans are different by describing their founding principles, political institutions, and early histories as colonies and then as nation-states on the North American continent. From the outset the differences were significant, and in the case of Canada deliberately different. Their differences remain important today.

In broad socio-historical terms, I believe there have been three phases in the trajectories of the two countries: opposite by design in the eighteenth and nineteenth centuries; tending toward convergence in the early twentieth century as the two countries built versions of the social welfare state, embraced materialism, fought together in two World Wars, collaborated with other allies in the subsequent Cold War, and developed affluent and increasingly hedonistic societies; and then divergence once again toward the end of the twentieth century and into the twenty-first.

The essential message of this book is that the social values of the two countries are once again becoming more distinct, not melding as conventional wisdom would have it. For several decades now Americans have been dismantling FDR's New Deal, while Canada has been struggling to make its public programs sustainable and to expand the rights and freedoms of its citizens. Canadians' values as consumers have evolved in post-material experiential directions, while the U.S. remains locked in modernity with its emphasis on money and the acquisition of material symbols of success on the social hierarchy.

More recently, the two countries' interests have also been diverging in the international sphere, which I think can be dated from the collapse of communism over a decade ago that left the United States as the world's only superpower. This formidable position reinforces America's penchant for survival-of-the-fittest social Darwinism and has inspired the U.S. government to abandon multilateralism for unilateralism, their opposition to the International Criminal Court being only one of many examples. America is returning to the Monroe Doctrine, only this time the U.S. claims a global sphere of influence and jurisdiction, not just the western hemisphere.

It is also clear from the trajectory of social change in Canada that the policies of cultural nationalism put in place over the past seventy-five years will not have the same resonance with average Canadians in the future as they have in the past. Canadians have become much less deferential to hierarchies and their leaders over the past half-century and are therefore less likely to allow nationalistic elites to define, regulate, and finance that uniqueness. The average Canadian wants access to all that the world has to offer, and much of that foreign content will be American. But unlike in the past, more autonomous, inner-directed Canadians wish to decide for themselves what they will consume and when.

The findings of this book have implications for public policy, consumer marketing, and human resources planning in Canada. In all instances, one must start from the premise that in many important ways the values of Canadians are different from those of Americans. You cannot speak to Canadians as if they were Americans, not just because it is politically incorrect but because they have different values and priorities and live in a very different context. *Globe and Mail* columnist Margaret Wente's post-9/11 declaration that "We are all Americans now" works as post-traumatic political rhetoric, but not as a statement of social scientific fact. Canadians may like Americans, speak the same language, and consume their fast food and popular culture, but we embrace a different hierarchy of values. Moreover, the differences, as I have attempted to show, are increasing rather than decreasing with economic integration.

"And then we are led to believe that they lived happily ever after."

Politicians and other marketers need to understand the unique trajectory of Canadian values and the often ambivalent attitude Canadians have to the United States. Neither a superficial pro- nor anti-Americanism will resonate with Canadians. Our research suggests a more subtle and nuanced orientation.

If my case for cultural divergence is at all convincing, and if readers agree that the values that motivate people are important, then the implications of our work are significant for Canada and for other nations in the world who fear the inevitable convergence of their values and cultures with that of the increasingly influential American empire. Canadians have sometimes reluctantly, but most often readily, welcomed American capital, technology, consumer products, and popular culture—and yet they have not adopted American values. If this is true for Canada, which is unquestionably the most Americanized country in the world, then it must be true for other modern and modernizing countries that find themselves being invaded by unarmed American forces.

Our data suggest the possibility of economic integration and strategic interdependence without the loss of cultural integrity and political sovereignty. This, I would argue, is because Canada's founding values, historical experiences, and political institutions are very different from those in the United States and have a greater influence on Canadians' contemporary values than the much vaunted forces of globalization.

Canadians, I believe, can continue to benefit from access to the American market and at the same time exercise political control with a considerable degree of latitude. Within fiscally prudent limits, our governments can tax or not tax whom they wish and at levels they choose; they can even impose a made-in-Canada tax like that on goods and services—the GST. Canada, I believe, can sustainably spend 40 to 45 per cent of its gross domestic product (GDP) on public goods and services, little of which is spent on the military, while its powerful southern neighbour spends less than a third of its GDP domestically, including the highest levels in the developed world on "defence."

There is also no reason to believe that Canada will not continue its trajectory of social liberalism even in the face of powerful forces of American social conservatism. As with the level of public sector expenditures, this makes Canada look more European than North American. But Canada is more than a peaceful microcosm of Europe; it is increasingly a peaceful microcosm of the entire world whose many interests and interdependencies are multipolar. Canada is becoming the home of a unique postmodern, postmaterial multiculturalism, generating hardy strains of new hybrids that will enrich this country and many others in the world.

Yes, there are clouds on the Canadian horizon. The recent retrenchment to a more traditional mindset, particularly among alienated youth, while pale in comparison to the nihilistic bent of American youth, cannot be lightly dismissed. These underdogs will become underwolves and they will bite back, hurting themselves and harming others if we cannot help them to find their way.

Throughout its history Canada has feared being absorbed into the United States, first by military force in the nineteenth century and then by market and cultural forces in the twentieth. What economists often fail to realize is that values matter most, and it is values, not material possessions once our basic needs are met, that give genuine meaning to people's lives.

My reading of Canadian values tells me that none has become more important in this country than autonomy—and that autonomy, in the context of interdependence, is valued at every level from the individual right up to the nation. Why would a people who are placing greater and greater emphasis on autonomy suddenly opt for dependence or absorption into a culture that is becoming increasingly alien to them? Besides, if the U.S. ever did seriously consider making Canada the fifty-first state, I am certain that after a period of due diligence and upon serious reflection Canadian values would make it an unacceptable acquisition. Can you imagine American conservatives allowing in their midst one huge Massachusetts?

SOCIAL VALUES METHODOLOGY

The Theoretical Foundations of Social Values Research

The underlying roots of our measurement system for both understanding the structure of social values in a society and then monitoring changes to them through time go back more than a century and a half to a curious young Frenchman named Alexis de Tocqueville. Tocqueville visited the United States in the 1830s in order to examine, first hand, the social and political life of the world's "first new nation." His *Democracy in America* is to social values research what Adam Smith's *The Wealth of Nations* is to the understanding of economics. Later in the nineteenth century, economist Thorstein Veblen took another giant step forward in the description and understanding of changes to human social values with his *Theory of the Leisure Class.*

A generation ago, academic social scientists such as Maslow, Riesman, Bell, Rokeach, and Thurstone began to describe and measure social values and explore the dynamics and impacts of them in their contemporary societies. They also identified a hierarchy of social values. For example, Maslow saw a structure and evolution of values from those associated with physical survival at the base level of human needs to those associated with self-actualization at the highest intellectual and moral levels of motivation. Individuals, and even whole societies, could be roughly characterized according to this values hierarchy depending on their predominant presenting beliefs and concerns.

In everyday parlance, the term "values" has come to take on a rich panoply of meanings and connotations, as for example the ubiquitous "family values," whose precise nature is often tacitly assumed despite it being a rather nebulous concept. In the 1960s, however, psychologist Milton Rokeach theorized about and defined social values in more precise scientific terms as having the following properties:

- they are beliefs;
- they are conceptions of, preferences for, and prescriptions about desirable modes of conduct or established orientations toward living and existence;
- they are conceptions of, preferences for, and prescriptions about desirable end-states of existence and social ideals.

Examples of the first type of beliefs, the means of living, include such values as honesty, hard work, and even "playing the system." Examples of the second type, the ends of living, include such values as status, health, peace, enlightenment, and power and influence.

Such formative and fundamental beliefs about the desirable means and ends of human conduct and existence are thought to be largely moulded in adolescence and early adulthood experience. Social values are informed by a person's prevalent perceptions and learnings, as attained through the family and close kinship group and by exposure to the predominant socio-historical environment and influences of the times into which he or she is born, is being raised, and comes of age (by which we mean "reaches sentient awareness of the world"). Once massively defined by such institutions as the Church and State, values have never been as idealistic or ideological as they were cast in Rokeach's view, but rather can also serve, quite pragmatically, as a person's or society's adaptation to, and justification of, current personal or cultural practices. Those practices—from interpersonal honesty to Machiavellianism, and from social assistance to genocide—are more often than not framed, or even "spun," in terms of the higher-order values they serve.

At Environics we consider values also to be evidence of "motivated cognition." These are beliefs that both determine and reflect our responses to the world as we struggle to meet such basic psychological and sociological needs as biological survival, connection with our close kinship groups, and our species' predilection for organizing socially in hierarchical and status-defined groups. So, beyond being desirable or prescribed means and ends of living, the concept of values has come to capture the deeper motivations behind human behaviour, tendencies of thought and feelings—unconscious as well as conscious—and the intra- and interpersonal dynamics related to them.

As we peel the onion of human motivation we see that a host of different aspects of people's thoughts and feelings about the world are well captured by an assessment of their "values," so defined. These aspects include expectancies, perceptions, and habits of thought; attitudes, judgments, and opinions; and intentions, tendencies, and actions. Values stand in, then, as a good description for a whole host of mental, emotional, and motivational postures and preparednesses (or "sets") with which we conduct our transactions with others and ourselves. What our research really attempts is a rather broadband analysis of the worldviews of individuals and of collectives, big and small.

THE EVOLUTION OF SOCIAL VALUES

For most of history the pace of change for us humans, culturally, technologically, and certainly spiritually, can only be described as glacial. A paradigm shift in worldviews happened rarely (think agriculture, iron, Christ, Galileo, Gutenberg, etc.) and its effects played out over generations of adaptation to the new invention of things or ideas. Not so in today's rapid world of invention and cultural convergence, where knowledge is discovered so rapidly that it can double within half a single generation. Now, the main mechanism for values change at a societal level is generational replacement. Youth are a constant source of new ideas and beliefs that infuse the culture and become predominant as the values of older generations wane with the death of each cohort.

Although shaped by the predominant experiences of the world in one's youth, values are not unchanging things set immutably in stone. Rather, they evolve through one's lifetime, albeit usually slowly. At the psychological level they change somewhat as a function of a person's life stage, life challenges, and experience. How many parents among us can deny an uncharacteristic but extreme authoritarian impulse or two when confronting a raging child? Moreover, values can change somewhat in response to major socio-historical events as they occur throughout people's lifespans; for example, in reaction to the spread of a technology like the PC or a disease like AIDS, as the result of insecurity born of a deep recession, the trauma of face-to-face combat in war, or in the chilling aftermath of an act of terror.

With the development of democracy and pluralism and the corresponding decline in unbending institutional regulation of people's worldviews in many parts of the planet, the character of values has changed—from one of high imposed stability and homogeneity within a culture and across time to one of flux and variability. And with the accelerated pace of change in most aspects of our world, this trend has been further magnified in current times.

Social Values Methodology

The social values assessment methodology we employ, which was first developed in the 1960s by Alain de Vulpian and our French colleagues at his company Cofremca in Paris, was invented in response to a wish to understand the evolution and meaning of the spontaneous rejection of traditional values and institutions evident among many young people in French society at that time. Like their North American colleagues in this enterprise, such as Daniel Yankelovich, the initial understanding of the societal structuring and evolution of social values came from extensive qualitative research, primarily through in-depth, one-on-one interviews. This research revealed new attitudes toward order, religious and secular authority, success, social status, the role of the sexes, and the place of youth in society, as well as a growing orientation of individuals toward personal autonomy, informality, and immediate gratification.

In the early 1970s, the knowledge gained from this qualitative research was used to create questions and scales designed to measure the diffusion of these new values within the French culture. This was accomplished through annual quantitative surveys of representative samples of the population. Thus was born the study of "socio-cultural currents"—the evolution of social values in a culture—and the resulting "Système Cofremca de Suivi des Courants Socio-Culturels" ("3SC"). The system was subsequently extended beyond France into more than twenty countries in Europe and the Americas. Our partner polling firm CROP, based in Quebec, imported 3SC to Canada in 1983, and, with the help of Environics Research Group and Kaagan Research Associates, into the United States in the 1990s. Outside of academic studies such as the World Values Survey based at the University of Michigan Survey Research Center, we believe that the 3SC-based system is the largest privately funded study of human social values currently conducted on the planet.

A Technical Look at the Social Values Map

Each new social values map we create for a culture requires about ten steps of detailed methodology leading up to a "trackable" quantitative analysis. Without going into the reasons why all these steps are necessary, nor how they are conducted statistically with the specific software algorithms we use, I set down these steps here and describe their most important facets in detail.

The goal of the first quantitative study in a new country is to understand the major structural relations among the values in evidence there. As more data come in, we begin to explore the currents and trajectories of values evolution in that society. Here are the necessary steps in the workup of a full-bodied socio-cultural profile of a society:

1. Values consultation and sensing
2. Questionnaire construction and testing
3. Survey sampling and fielding
4. Data cleaning and treatment
5. Values exploration and extraction
6. Values indexing and reliability testing
7. Respondent classification into strong or weak expression of the values
8. Perceptual mapping and anchoring

9. Solution integration and labelling
10. Inferencing and storytelling

Step 1

Values sensing is the key to developing a socio-cultural analysis for any country, for this is where we discover what is existing and prevalent, and in later researches what is new, in a society. Through the qualitative research we routinely conduct in a given culture, we constantly seek to extract and abstract what is novel and potentially important in relation to that which has come before. We ask what is bubbling up from the many generative groups in the culture, from youth and new immigrant groups to emerging political or religious movements. We try to sniff out what is developing in terms of political counterculture, new ideologies, technology uptake and resistance, new social forms in the family, changing attitudes toward work, trends in popular culture and entertainment, evolving patterns of consumption, emerging preferences for travel and leisure, new aesthetic and design sensibilities, evolving food and drink preferences, and so forth.

We also conduct special studies wherein we find the opinion leaders, local experts, and market mavens at the sharp edge of the values change wedge and then interview them in depth. Added to the mix are Web-based research, anthropological studies called everyday life researches (EDLs), and countless focus groups with both average and exceptional people. We interview local cultural experts, commentators, and interpreters, and lean on our international colleagues, who also conduct this type of research worldwide, for their experiences and insights. When our preparation is complete, we sift through the trends collaboratively—through the benefits and biases of our individual training as sociologists and semioticians, psychologists and marketer researchers, prognosticators and communicators.

In our "search for the new," we look for what is likely to be enduring rather than faddish in cultural evolution; current fashion and hot-this-season children's toys, for example, are not viewed as constituting what we take to be values. Plus, we look for things that are likely to have multiple manifestations in people's lives. In recent years, for example, the perceived invasiveness of employers, governments, and e-commerce marketers has led to an increasing concern for privacy that is likely to find various expressions as people assert their rights to privacy across a wider spectrum of their lives. We would predict that these tendencies—already in evidence among the society's leading edge "sensitives," who are quick to read and respond to emerging social realities—have a good chance of diffusing more generally throughout the culture. But we may be wrong! Only time and empirical data will tell whether, or under what conditions, people will accept or reject such privacy threats as mandatory drug testing, workplace video monitoring, or e-commerce "leave behinds." To find out which way the cookie crumbles, indeed if it does at all, we need a quantitative survey to assess our hunches, heuristics, and hypotheses about the supposed multiple manifestations of each value.

Steps 2 to 4

The first quantitative stage in the analysis is a familiar one in survey research: to develop and administer a high-quality survey to a representative sampling of the society's population so that valid inferences can be drawn, robust data patterns can be replicated, and confident generalizations can be made about various subgroups in the population. This requires steps 2 to 4 in our list above. The goal is to translate the subtle and not-so-subtle values and mental postures we have sensed in step 1 into a set of empirical measures that are valid and reliable, replicable and defensible. This is where science and art really begin to commingle in our work, and where, if we are any good at what we do, the solid scientific methodology underlying our values measurement system will be artfully conceived, crafted, and carried off.

Steps 5 to 7

Steps 5 to 7 represent the heart of the analysis. It is here that we both validate our hypothesized social values and discover new values that emerge from the data, using a multivariate statistical technique called principal components analysis (PCA) combined with Cronbach alpha reliability analysis. At the end of these steps we hope to have articulated a set of social values that adequately describes the culture under investigation, and from which meaningful and interesting insights can be drawn. For the United States and Canada we typically assess and track about 100 such values, from those with grand and enduring sociological stature, such as *Need for Status Recognition, Obedience to Authority,* and *Sexism,* to those that describe the subtle, immediate concerns of living, such as *Concern for Appearance, Meaningful Moments,* and *Discerning Hedonism.* Through such disparate content we are better able to capture people's mental, emotional, spiritual, and behavioural expectations and response tendencies, and thus discern the phenomenology of their everyday lives.

Each value comprises the measurement and combination of several survey items in its construction. For example, *Global Consciousness* is defined as: Considering oneself a "citizen of the world" first and foremost, over a "citizen of one's community and country," combined with a certain degree of non-ethnocentricity, a feeling of affinity with peoples in all countries.

This idea is measured by having respondents agree or disagree on a four-point scale with several items in the survey, such as "I feel that I am more a citizen of the world than a citizen of my country." The items are combined mathematically to create this value measure, scores are assigned to each respondent on this and all other values, and those respondents scoring highest (or sometimes lowest) on a value are classified as strong (or weak) in evidencing that tendency.

Steps 8 to 9

In steps 8 and 9, we again use principal components analysis (PCA), or sometimes factor analysis of correspondence (FAC), to explore the associations between individuals' standing on their many social values. From this analysis emerges a "mapspace solution," a set of axes or dimensions that more generally underlie, differentiate, and explain the collection of values we have assessed among our respondents. Many such solutions are possible and considered. The axes chosen should allow us to interpret the values together on one common map, to explore their relative positions with other values, and to track their movements through time in a compelling way. The axes are named to capture the main themes of the values and mental postures that define them. While there are typically three to seven axes that best describe the interrelations among the 100-plus values we have assessed in our respondents, we usually depict the data in only the two most explanatory and interesting dimensions when explicating our findings.

It is important to remember that our map is about the *people* who are plotted there. Individuals are assigned a set of axis coordinates on the various dimensions and we use these to plot each individual, or the average positions of subgroups of respondents, or the entire population average of a culture, or of that culture at a specific point in time. The axes are chosen, in part, when the anchorings provided by plotting major demographic subgroups make fundamental sense across the values space (for example, older age should be associated with greater conformity, and higher education with autonomy). But this is not our sole criterion for selecting the axes.

It is worth keeping in mind that any type of group, demographic or not, can be defined and plotted on the map, as for example

- teenagers;
- women;
- high household income earners;
- Midwesterners;
- generational cohorts, such as Baby Boomers;
- supporters of a political party or position;
- early adopters of a technology;
- heavy Brand X users;
- "somewhat satisfied" customers;
- dog owners;
- particularly strong believers in the value of *Ethical Consumerism*.

The last example is of particular interest. In order to create the map that positions the 100 social values in the mapspace, we adopt the following convention. We place the name of each value we assess at the point on the map where its strongest proponents reside. We define "strongest proponents" as approximately the top one-fifth of people who report that they agree with the value (as assessed by all its items combined). In other words, the label "Ethical Consumerism" is positioned on the map by proxy, at the average axes position points of those 20 per cent of individuals strongest in their orientation toward this value, which we establish by asking how much they monitor their consumption and buy from companies with good track records in environmental and employee practice.

Each of the groups listed above can also be profiled in detail on the basis of all their values to see what their particularly strong and weak value orientations are among the 100 we assess. It is usually the case that a complex array of value standings characterizes any one group, for example the highly educated, but in total they must combine to give the average position for the group we show on our two major values axes. In our proprietary work, we compute a set of scores for all 100 values that indexes how much stronger or weaker a chosen group is compared with the national average (or any other particular comparison group of interest). The resulting "gestalt" of correlated value orientations for that group provides a rich portrait that can be used for understanding and communicating with them.

As described in the body of this book, our analysis of North Americans has revealed three major structural axes that can be used to portray the values of the peoples of the United States and Canada (the solution is of course driven by the American axes, given the nearly 10:1 population ratio between our two societies):

- survival versus fulfillment;
- authority versus individuality;
- change orientation (openness versus resistance to change).

These axes capture the organization of the values we assess when we consider them as a whole, and the resulting quadrants of this map (described elsewhere in this book) provide a good representation of the major *structure* of the values shared by a people. That there have been notable movements on each of these axes in the past decade also makes them very useful in telling the *dynamic* story of social values evolution in North America. For example, the position points of various groups (youth, the religious right, Hispanics, etc.) can be examined as they shift through time, and their group profiles can be studied over the years to determine the changes in their overall social values portraits. Indeed, we can even plot the evolution and trajectories of entire societies and cultures.

This axes framework is further enhanced by comparison of our work to ongoing qualitative and quantitative research studies conducted world-wide that probe the evolution of values and their meaning in many other cultures. We can describe not only the culture-specific manifestations of social values that differentiate societies but also the commonalities that bind us cross-culturally in the human experience. The axes of social change that emerge from the socio-cultural analysis in Canada and the U.S. are congruent with those that social scientists have discerned in other continents and in other cultures—an encouraging conceptual replication of our work that, despite local variations in history, politics, religion, and social forms, speaks to the universality of human values and to the common set of life challenges we face as a species.

Step 10

Once the primary map, descriptive of the structure and dynamics of values and their evolution, is set for a culture, our fun really begins. For it is in step 10 that we get to use our map for understanding people's values in much more depth, and for helping our clients (the people who pay the bills) to do so. There are typically many surprises as we plumb the depths of people's worldviews and motivations, and much subtlety as well.

What do men and women have in common in social values, how are they different, and how are they changing? What are the values and worldviews associated with achieving a higher level of education? What are the in-depth values profiles of old people and young people, Albertans and Nova Scotians, New Englanders and Texarkansans, professionals and unionists, Catholics and Protestants? What are the differences in mental postures of people who vote Liberal versus Alliance, are Democrats or Republicans, jog versus bird-watch in their spare time, buy Toyotas versus Fords, drink Coke versus Pepsi, read *The New Yorker* versus *Chatelaine,* believe in angels or are atheists, run PCs versus Macs? What does the wider study of values tell us about the people in our society who are most accepting of violence, who are opting for voluntary simplicity in their lifestyles, or who are highly entrepreneurial?

Social values provide clues to each of these questions, and many more. Perhaps our system's greatest contribution comes from its ability to identify the basic mindsets that are emerging in our culture as well as globally. Are these the mindsets that we should be teaching our children in order to prepare them for the new millennium? We think yes, but such a self-laudatory statement about "our contribution" is only possible if, like us, you judge *Adaptive Navigation* to be a preferred and desirable means of charting the course to your goals in life.

TREND GLOSSARY[1]

ACCEPTANCE OF VIOLENCE People highest on this trend believe that violence is an inevitable fact of life that must be accepted with a certain degree of indifference. Belief that violence can be both cathartic and persuasive.

ACTIVE GOVERNMENT Tendency to believe that government efficaciously performs socially beneficial functions. A desire for more government involvement in resolving social issues.

ADAPTABILITY TO COMPLEXITY (REVERSE OF AVERSION TO COMPLEXITY) Tendency to adapt easily to the uncertainties of modern life and not to feel threatened by the changes and complexities of society today. A desire to explore this complexity as a learning experience and a source of opportunity.

ADAPTIVE NAVIGATION Having the flexibility to adapt to unforeseen events that interfere with the realization of one's goals. Being flexible in defining one's expectations and ways of meeting one's objectives.

ADVERTISING AS STIMULUS Tendency to enjoy viewing advertising for its aesthetic properties; to enjoy advertising in a wide range of venues, from magazines to television to outdoor signs and billboards.

AMERICAN DREAM The belief that the United States is the "land of opportunity" and that anyone can make it, and make it big, if they try hard enough. The belief that even in middle age, one can start anew, launching new initiatives or changing one's way of life.

ANOMIE AND AIMLESSNESS The feeling of having no goals in life. Experiencing a void of meaning with respect to life in general. A feeling

---

1. These trends are tracked in the United States. Trends followed only in Canada are defined in Appendix F.

of alienation from society, having the impression of being cut off from what's happening.

ATTRACTION TO CROWDS Enjoyment of being in large crowds as a means of deindividualization and connection-seeking.

AVERSION TO COMPLEXITY (REVERSE OF ADAPTABILITY TO COMPLEXITY)
A desire to keep one's life simple and predictable. People strong on this trend are intimidated and threatened by the changes in society and the complexities of modern life. They seek stability and simplicity.

BRAND APATHY (REVERSE OF IMPORTANCE OF BRAND) Placing little importance on the brand name of a product.

BUYING ON IMPULSE (REVERSE OF DISCRIMINATING CONSUMERISM)
Tendency to purchase products on impulse, enticed by exciting advertising or packaging. Rarely seeking out information on products before buying.

CELEBRATING PASSAGES A need to perform certain rituals or small acts to demarcate the passing of various phases of one's life. A desire to celebrate traditional passages (e.g., birth, marriage, death) or invent new ones.

CIVIC APATHY (REVERSE OF CIVIC ENGAGEMENT) Reflects a disinterest in the political process and participation in the democratic process. Recognition of the division of society between the "haves" and the "have-nots," and a willingness to accept the inevitability of the status quo.

CIVIC ENGAGEMENT (REVERSE OF CIVIC APATHY) A belief that active involvement in the political process can make a difference in society. People strongest on this trend reject the notion that inequities in society are inevitable and should be expected.

COMMUNITY INVOLVEMENT Measure of the interest in what's happening in one's neighbourhood, city, town, or region. Reflected in activities ranging from reading the weekly community newspaper to socio-political involvement in community organizations.

CONCERN FOR APPEARANCE Placing a great deal of importance on appearing "attractive" and concerned about the image projected by one's appearance. People who are strong on this trend are image-driven.

CONFIDENCE IN ADVERTISING (REVERSE OF SKEPTICISM OF ADVERTISING)
Tendency to trust and use advertising as a source of reliable information. Also, a tendency to identify with the fashions and the role models promoted by advertising and the consumer society.

CONFIDENCE IN BIG BUSINESS The belief that big businesses strive to strike a fair balance between making a profit and working in the public's interest. People who score high on this trend express a certain level of faith that what serves the interest of big business also serves the interest of society, and vice versa. Associating good quality and service with big companies and well-known products.

CONFIDENCE IN SMALL BUSINESS Confidence in the commitment of small-business owners to the provision of quality goods and services. Belief that small-business owners are not just profit-driven.

CULTURAL ASSIMILATION (REVERSE OF MULTICULTURALISM) *E Pluribus Unum.* Belief that people should adopt a culture that is "American" first and foremost. Believing that in coming to America, immigrants should let go of their languages and customs and embrace the American way of life.

CULTURE SAMPLING This trend identifies the view that other cultures have a great deal to teach us, and measures people's inclination to incorporate some of these cultural influences into their own lives.

DISCERNING HEDONISM The capacity to savour pleasures; the appreciation of complex emotions and the ability to link enjoyment to other realms of experience in everyday life.

DISCRIMINATING CONSUMERISM (REVERSE OF BUYING ON IMPULSE) Seeking objective, comparative product information and carefully evaluating one's needs before making purchases. Preference for practical and functional products, satisfying real needs.

DUTY Belief that duties and obligations to others should be fulfilled before turning to one's personal pleasures and interests.

ECOLOGICAL CONCERN (REVERSE OF ECOLOGICAL FATALISM) A tendency to believe that today's environmental problems are a result of industrial and personal disregard for the environment. These people feel that the trend toward environmental destruction is unacceptable and reject the notion that job protection or economic advancement should be allowed at the expense of environmental protection.

ECOLOGICAL FATALISM (REVERSE OF ECOLOGICAL CONCERN) People highest on this trend believe that some amount of pollution is unavoidable in industrial societies and accept it as a part of life. They feel that there is little they can do to change this fact.

EFFORT TOWARD HEALTH The commitment to focus on diet and exercise in order to feel better and have a healthy, wholesome lifestyle. A willingness to transform one's lifestyle through exercise and radical changes to diet.

EMOTIONAL CONTROL (REVERSE OF PURSUIT OF INTENSITY) A propensity to give priority to reason as the principal way of understanding life. A desire to keep one's emotional life "on an even keel"; to use logic and reason to control one's feelings and emotions and to base day-to-day decisions on reason and logic. A reluctance to experience or express emotions.

ENTHUSIASM FOR NEW TECHNOLOGY Fascination with the possibilities offered by modern technology; seeking information about the latest products and innovations. Excitement about the ways technology can better their lives.

ENTREPRENEURIALISM Taking steps to fulfill the dream of becoming self-employed, rather than being a 9-to-5 employee. Feeling that the freedom and opportunity that comes with owning one's own business is more rewarding than working for someone else.

EQUAL RELATIONSHIP WITH YOUTH Breaking down traditional hierarchical and patriarchal relationships by giving youth equal freedoms to those of adults. Discipline issued by adults over young people is therefore replaced by freedom and increased individualism.

ETHICAL CONSUMERISM A focus on the perceived ethical and social responsibility policies and practices of the companies from which they buy. Consideration of labour policies, mistreatment of animals, etc. Desire to see companies be good corporate citizens in terms of these social concerns.

EVERYDAY ETHICS A measure of how individuals respond in situations that put their ethical beliefs to the test. When a person sees a way of turning a situation to their advantage at the expense of another person, institution, or company, how do they respond? Will they report mistakes made in their favour by a waiter, a bank, or the government?

EVERYDAY RAGE A willingness to express anger and dissatisfaction toward others. This ranges from a refusal to accept bad service to arguing with others in public or even engaging in "road rage." Implicit in this is a feeling that people can no longer expect fair treatment by being polite or quiet.

FAITH IN SCIENCE The belief that science and technology can work in a positive way by expanding natural resources to meet future demand, and that new technologies can repair past damage to the natural world. Excitement in the possibilities offered by new technologies and modern medicine.

FATALISM (REVERSE OF PERSONAL CONTROL) The tendency to believe that one's life is shaped by forces beyond one's control. Feeling unconcerned with trying to change the inevitable direction of one's life.

FEAR OF VIOLENCE Fear of violence occurring in today's society. Feeling insecure about personal safety; feeling vulnerable to attack in the city or in one's neighbourhood, especially at night. Tendency to believe that one must be on constant alert against gratuitous violence.

FINANCIAL SECURITY A feeling of security and optimism about one's financial future. A sense of being personally responsible for and in control of one's financial situation.

FLEXIBLE FAMILIES (REVERSE OF TRADITIONAL FAMILIES) Willingness to accept non-traditional definitions of family, such as common-law and same-sex marriages. The belief that family should be defined by emotional links rather than by legal formalities or institutions. The belief that society should be open to new definitions of what constitutes a family.

FLEXIBLE GENDER IDENTITY (REVERSE OF TRADITIONAL GENDER IDENTITY) The feeling that one has both a feminine and masculine side to one's personality. The desire to actively explore and express these different facets of one's personality. Having a feeling of being more masculine at times and more feminine at others.

GENDER PARITY Seeking fairness and equal treatment for men and women in work roles. A desire to transcend sexual stereotypes and to see an end to discrimination, tempered by a belief that a job should go to the best candidate, man or woman, rather than employing reverse discrimination to achieve equal representation of men and women in all professions.

GLOBAL CONSCIOUSNESS (REVERSE OF PAROCHIALISM) Considering oneself a "citizen of the world" first and foremost, over a "citizen of one's community and country." Non-ethnocentricity; feeling affinity to peoples in all countries.

HETERARCHY Tendency to think that leadership in organizations should be flexible and fluid; that a single leader should not take control of everything and that initiatives and leadership should emerge from different individuals as a function of their strengths. A belief that teamwork is more effective than autocracy.

HOLISTIC HEALTH Taking a holistic approach to health and well-being. Individuals who are high on this trend are sensitive to the linkage between their mental, spiritual, and physical well-being. They feel that they can exert control over their health and that the choices they make today will pay off in later years.

IMPORTANCE OF AESTHETICS Tendency to base purchase decisions on aesthetic rather than utilitarian considerations. Measures the attention given to the beauty of objects and products purchased. People strong on this trend often buy products purely for their appearance.

IMPORTANCE OF BRAND (REVERSE OF BRAND APATHY) Giving great weight to the brand name of a product or service; a tendency to have favourite brands.

IMPORTANCE OF SPONTANEITY Tendency to enthusiastically embrace the unexpected and spontaneous events that temporarily interrupt daily routines.

INTEREST IN THE MYSTERIOUS Tendency to reject the assumption that all valid knowledge must be logical, rational, or scientific in favour of an acceptance of beliefs or phenomena that remain mysterious or unexplained by modern science.

INTROSPECTION AND EMPATHY Tendency to analyze and examine one's actions and those of others, rather than being judgmental about variances from the norm or from one's own way of doing things. An interest in understanding life rather than taking sides.

INTUITION AND IMPULSE A way of understanding and transacting with the world that largely leaves aside controlled and critical rational thought. A tendency to be guided less by reason and ideology than by one's own emotions and feelings. Impulsive and spontaneous; able to change one's opinions easily.

JOY OF CONSUMPTION Intense gratification through the purchase of consumer goods (rather than basic necessities). Enjoying consumption for the pleasure of consumption. People who are strong on this trend are often more excited by the act of buying than by the use of the products they buy.

JUST DESERTS Confidence that, in the end, people get what they deserve as a result of the decisions they make, both positively and negatively.

LARGESSE OBLIGE Social conscience of the economic variety. The haves have a moral duty to help or share with the have-nots.

LIVING VIRTUALLY People strong on this trend are spending an increasing amount of time watching TV, using computers, or at the movies. Reflects a more virtual than real connection to the world.

LOOK GOOD FEEL GOOD A belief that, by taking care to look one's best, one will feel and project confidence, thereby helping to achieve one's goals in life.

MEANINGFUL MOMENTS Cherishing the ordinary moments in everyday life over once-in-a-lifetime, grand-scale events. Taking time to indulge in individual pleasures. The sense of impermanence that accompanies momentary connections with others does not diminish the value of the moment.

MORE POWER FOR BUSINESS Belief that business institutions (e.g., banks, foreign companies) should have a greater influence in society.

MORE POWER FOR MEDIA Belief that celebrities and those in the media should have a greater influence in society.

MORE POWER FOR POLITICS Belief that government institutions and political parties should have a greater influence in society.

MULTICULTURALISM (REVERSE OF CULTURAL ASSIMILATION) Openness toward the diverse cultures, ethnic communities, and immigrants that make up America. A belief that ethnic groups should be encouraged to preserve their cultural identities, and that others should seek to learn about them.

MYSTERIOUS FORCES The impression that forces greater than ourselves control our destiny and that mysterious forces that we cannot understand affect our lives.

NATIONAL PRIDE Defining one's identity through national pride and believing that America should hold a strong position in the world.

NEED FOR STATUS RECOGNITION Desire to be held in esteem and respect by others, and to express one's social standing or aspired status, through a display of fine manners, good taste, style, or "chic."

NETWORKING The desire to assemble a diverse network of friends and associations based on one's own personal interests. Often these friends and associations will have little in common with one another, apart from the fact that they are all connected to one's own interests.

OBEDIENCE TO AUTHORITY (REVERSE OF REJECTION OF AUTHORITY) A belief in playing by the rules. The belief that persons or organizations in positions of authority should be deferred to at all times. There are rules in society and everyone should follow them. Feeling that young people in particular should be taught to obey authority rather than question it.

OSTENTATIOUS CONSUMPTION Desire to impress others and express one's social standing through the display of objects that symbolize affluence.

PAROCHIALISM (REVERSE OF GLOBAL CONSCIOUSNESS) Feeling of connectedness to one's town, city, region, or country. A disregard for what is happening in other countries, and a preference for seeing symbols of home, such as a McDonalds restaurant, when travelling abroad.

PATRIARCHY Belief that "the father of the family must be the master in his own home."

PENCHANT FOR RISK Desire to take risks in order to get what one wants out of life. Also, indulging in dangerous and forbidden activities for their associated emotional high.

PERSONAL CHALLENGE Setting difficult goals, even if just to prove to themselves that they can do it. People strong on this trend finish what they start, persevering until their self-assigned task is completed to their satisfaction. Rejecting personal failure.

PERSONAL CONTROL (REVERSE OF FATALISM) Striving to organize and control the direction of one's future, even when it feels that there are forces beyond one's immediate control.

PERSONAL CREATIVITY Desire to use one's imagination and creative talents in daily life, both at work and at play.

PERSONAL ESCAPE Interest in mystery, romanticism, and adventure, as a means of distracting oneself from everyday challenges and burdens. People strongest on this trend feel that their dreams and imagination are important driving forces in their daily lives; they long for that which is beyond the practical and desire to experience beauty and pleasure in surprise and astonishment.

PERSONAL EXPRESSION The desire to develop and express one's personality, combined with a desire to communicate in an authentic and sincere manner with others.

PRIMACY OF THE FAMILY Centrality of family; making personal sacrifices and providing for one's children over all else.

PROPRIETY The importance of dressing so as not to give offence, but rather to elicit and communicate respect in more formal relationships, in public, and at work. Behaving in a way that respects oneself and others. A preference for the formal over the casual.

PROTECTION OF PRIVACY Great concern about the fact that, through databases and other means, government and business are amassing increasingly large banks of information about people's private lives.

PURSUIT OF INTENSITY (REVERSE OF EMOTIONAL CONTROL) Desire to live intensely. Also, a tendency to be guided less by reason and ideology than by one's own emotions, feelings, and intuition. A need to constantly experience new sensations.

RACIAL FUSION People who are strongest on this trend are accepting of ethnic diversity within families, such as interracial marriage, believing that it enriches people's lives.

REJECTION OF AUTHORITY (REVERSE OF OBEDIENCE TO AUTHORITY) Desire to transcend the rigid framework of traditional authority. Possessing a questioning orientation, critical of and willing to look beyond the status quo.

REJECTION OF ORDER Living with a certain amount of disorder as an expression of oneself. Also, a desire to distance oneself from society's traditional moral code governing good manners and the golden rule in favour of a more informal and relaxed approach to life.

RELIGION À LA CARTE A selective, personal, adaptive, and eclectic approach to the adoption of religious beliefs. Spiritually questing; seeking personal fulfillment through learning about other faiths.

RELIGIOSITY Placing great importance on religion as a construct that guides one's life. Also, placing great significance on having an affiliation with an organized religious faith. Tendency to consider that religion represents the essential values and education that should be transmitted to the next generation.

SAVING ON PRINCIPLE The tendency to save and accumulate money, motivated by a moral impulse for future security. A preference for frugality and denial to self of "luxuries." Displaying tendencies toward inhibition.

SEARCH FOR ROOTS Desire to preserve and maintain one's cultural and ethnic roots and to live in accordance with one's own traditions and customs. Also, a yearning to return to one's cultural roots in order to rediscover and participate in the fundamental values that give meaning to one's life.

SELECTIVE USE OF PERSONAL SERVICES Deferring to experts for advice when needed, but maintaining contact with them. Those highest on this trend seek opportunities to learn from them or even play an active role in the decision-making process.

SENSUALISM Tendency to give priority to the sensorial perceptions aroused by the non-visual senses. A more sensual, intuitive, and affective approach to life.

SEXISM Belief that "the father of the family must be the master in his own home." Believing in traditional, male-dominated views on the division of gender roles—that men are naturally superior to women. These views carry into economic issues, such as the belief that, when both partners are working, the husband should be the main breadwinner.

SEXUAL PERMISSIVENESS A tendency to be sexually permissive regarding oneself and others. Fidelity within marriage or between partners and the prohibition of premarital sex are of little importance.

SKEPTICISM OF ADVERTISING (REVERSE OF CONFIDENCE IN ADVERTISING) Distrust that advertising messages are truthful or even helpful for making purchasing decisions.

SOCIAL INTIMACY A desire to be around and connect with smaller, closely knit groups of people. Feeling that smaller organizations are better than larger ones.

SOCIAL RESPONSIBILITY A belief that society, and the individual, have a responsibility to help those less fortunate. Tendency to believe that quality of life can improve when people work together.

SPIRITUAL QUEST A desire for an intense spiritual life; contemplating questions of existence and meaning.

TECHNOLOGY ANXIETY People strong on this trend are intimidated and threatened by technological changes and express much concern about the ethical and moral implications of scientific advances

TIME STRESS Feeling overwhelmed by the demands on one's time. A desire to obtain better control of one's life stress, particularly as it applies to better time management.

TRADITIONAL FAMILY (REVERSE OF FLEXIBLE FAMILY) Defining "family" in traditional terms as a man and a woman who are married with children. Unwilling to expand the traditional concept of family beyond the legal formality of a marriage licence to include same-sex couples or unmarried couples.

TRADITIONAL GENDER IDENTITY (REVERSE OF FLEXIBLE GENDER IDENTITY) The belief that normal gender behaviour is clearly delineated—men are masculine and women are feminine; that men and women have particular characteristics inherent in their gender. The rejection of the notion that masculine and feminine behaviours and roles can, or should, cross the traditional gender line.

VITALITY The sense that one has a great deal of energy and is in contact with this energy. Measures an energetic, lively approach to life, a feeling that one has more vigour and initiative than most other people.

VOLUNTARY SIMPLICITY Balancing quality versus quantity in life. The desire to achieve a sense of quality of life combined with the willingness to scale back one's material expectations or concentrate on those things that are truly important in life.

WORK ETHIC Following the golden rule and guiding one's life according to the principles of deferring pleasure in order to realize greater gains in the future. Individuals who score high on this trend believe that children should be taught to work hard in order to get ahead.

XENOPHOBIA The sense that too much immigration threatens the purity of the country. The belief that immigrants who have made their new home in the United States should set aside their cultural backgrounds and blend into "the American melting pot."

LIST OF FIGURES

COMPOSITION OF U.S. REGIONS

Regions	New England	Mid Atlantic	South Atlantic	Midwest	Deep South	Plains	Texarkan	Mountain	Pacific
States	Maine	New York	Delaware	Ohio	Tennessee	Minnesota	Arkansas	Montana	Washington
	New Hampshire	New Jersey	DC	Kentucky	Alabama	North Dakota	Oklahoma	Idaho	Oregon
	Vermont	Pennsylvania	Maryland	Michigan	Mississippi	South Dakota	Louisiana	Wyoming	California
	Massachusetts	West Virginia	Virginia	Indiana		Iowa	Texas	Colorado	
	Connecticut		North Carolina	Wisconsin		Nebraska		Utah	
	Rhode Island		South Carolina	Illinois		Missouri		Nevada	
			Georgia			Kansas		New Mexico	
			Florida					Arizona	

AMERICAN/NORTH AMERICAN SOCIO-CULTURAL MAPS

E1

The Status and Security Quadrant

AUTHORITY

Obedience to Authority

Work Ethic
Traditional Gender Identity

Patriarchy

Trust in Personal Advisors
Personal Challenge
Look Good Feel Good

Technology Anxiety
Confidence in Small Business
Confidence in Advertising
Need for Status Recognition
Community Involvement
Xenophobia Importance of Brand
Saving on Principle

SURVIVAL

E2

The Authenticity and Responsibilty Quadrant

AUTHORITY

Traditional Family

Religiosity

Propriety

National Pride
Primacy of the Family   Everyday Ethics
          Duty

                    Meaningful Moments
          Effort Toward Health
   Social Responsibility   Discriminating Consumerism
Social Intimacy   Spiritual Quest
American Dream
          Cultural Assimilation
          Holistic Health
   Concern for Appearance   Gender Parity
Aversion to Complexity
          Ethical Consumerism   Introspection & Empathy

FULFILLMENT

E3

The Idealism and Autonomy Quadrant

Heterarchy   Entrepeneurialism   Ecological Concern

Cultural Sampling   Brand Apathy

Personal Control

Importance of Spontaneity

Adaptability to Complexity

Interest in the Mysterious   Rejection of Order

Global Consciousness   Personal Creativity

Religion à la Carte

Flexible Gender Identity

Flexible Families

Equal Relationship with Youth   Rejection of Authority

FULFILLMENT

INDIVIDUALITY

E4

The Exclusion and Intensity Quadrant

SURVIVAL

Sexism   Fatalism   Intuition & Impulse
           Importance of Aesthetics   Financial Security
Confidence in Big Business   Pursuit of Intensity
  Just Deserts   Personal Escape
           Enthusiasm for New Technology
      Ostentatious Consumption
    Active Government
    Living Virtually   Multiculturalism   Buying on Impulse
    Everyday Rage   More Power for Business
Civic Apathy
                    Racial Fusion
  Anomie and Aimlessness

           Penchant for Risk

Acceptance of Violence

           Sexual Permissiveness

INDIVIDUALITY

E5

U.S. Quadrant Evolutions
1992, 1996, 2000

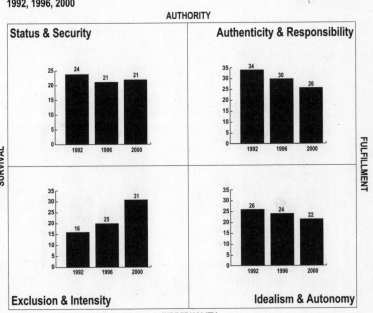

E6

Canada Quadrant Evolutions
1992, 1996, 2000

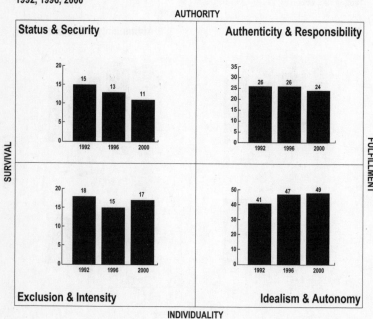

E7

Americans and Canadians Over 60 on the Socio-Cultural Map

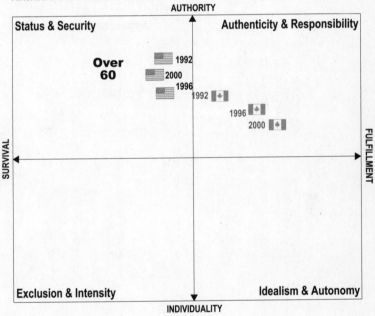

E8

Americans and Canadians 45 to 59 on the Socio-Cultural Map

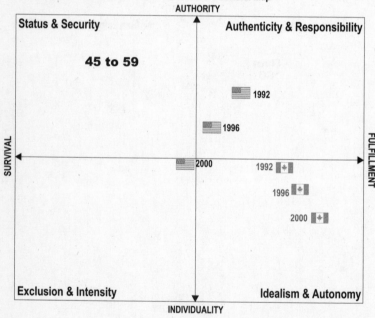

E9

Americans and Canadians 30 to 44 on the Socio-Cultural Map

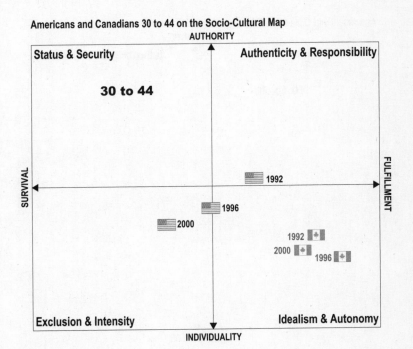

E10

Americans and Canadians 20 to 29 on the Socio-Cultural Map

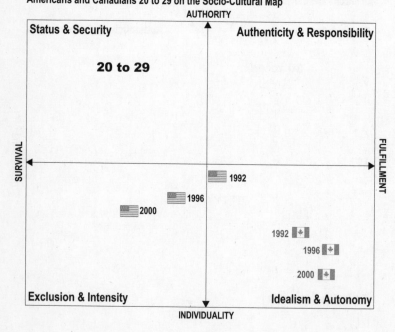

E11

Americans and Canadians Under 20 on the Socio-Cultural Map

E12

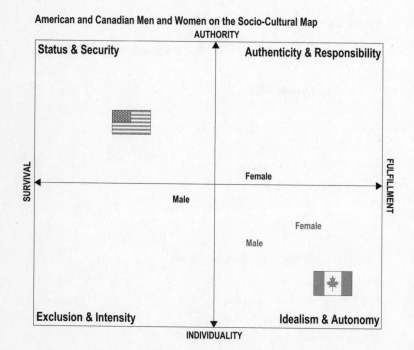

American and Canadian Men and Women on the Socio-Cultural Map

THE CANADIAN SOCIO-CULTURAL MAP AND FIGURES

The layout of the Canadian socio-cultural mapspace is determined by respondents' answers to our survey questions. Any given trend's location on the social values map is dictated by its positive or negative correlation with other trends on the map. Trends that are positively correlated will appear close together on the map, and those that are negatively correlated will appear far apart.

The Canadian socio-cultural map is substantially different from the American map explored in Chapter One, since each map is developed from a very large number of questions designed to measure and track a large number of values in each society. Some questions and values are unique to a particular society, others are common to a number of societies, and still more to all societies we have studied. We do not take a template constructed in one society and impose it willy-nilly on each subsequent culture we investigate. Rather, each society is studied on its own terms, borrowing as much as possible from previous research elsewhere and adding new questions over time that tap emerging values and trends.

In the case of Canada and the United States, about half the questions and values are the same. This substantial overlap enables us to easily compare the two societies over time, as we have done in the body of this book. The remaining questions, which differ in the two countries, contribute to producing a socio-cultural map for Canada that is distinct from the U.S. map. The axes and quadrants of the Canadian map are different from those I discussed in Chapter One, thus the need for this appendix. More importantly, the socio-cultural differences between the two societies also mean that the response patterns on, and correlations between, our questions and values produce a different structuring of the values axes for each country.

For example, on the Canadian map, the trends *Religiosity* and *Interest in the Mysterious* are nearly on top of each other (see figure on page 192). On the United States map, by contrast, the two trends are separated by half the length of the vertical axis (see Figures E2 and E3). The correlation of the two trends in Canada suggests that here religion is perceived more as a means of confronting the mysterious aspects of our lives and of building into our daily routines some practice (attendance at religious services, prayer, study of sacred texts) that honours the great imponderables of existence. The fact that these two trends are relatively far apart on the U.S. map (with *Religiosity* near the top, where the trends associated with rules, order, and authority tend to be, and *Interest in the Mysterious* farther down, among more autonomy-oriented trends such as *Heterarchy* and *Adaptive Navigation*) suggests that Americans who register high levels of religiosity are more likely to see religion as a way of *eliminating* rather than exploring mystery. Our hypothesis is that Americans are more likely than Canadians to see religion as a source of strong moralist narratives and strict rules for personal conduct that, although sometimes difficult to follow, guarantee bliss in the hereafter. This orientation to religion sees it as one big answer rather than as a collection of venerable questions. In America, our data suggest, religion is the end of dialogue, not its beginning, almost a retreat from other points of view rather than an effort to understand and accommodate them.

Although there is much more to say about both these trends, this example offers a glimpse of how correlations among trends tend to enrich our understanding of the trends themselves. It also illustrates how differences between the actual mapspaces belonging to Canada and the United States offer a grounding for our interpretation of the differences between the two societies.

Turning our attention now to the Canadian map, our first step is to gain a sense of the map's axes and quadrants in order to understand what Canadians' positions and movements on the map imply in terms of social change. The horizontal axis is one of inner- and outer-directedness. On the right side of the map, the inner-directed side, we find values that indicate a tendency to live life by one's own lights rather than according to the expectations of others. Superficially, inner-directedness suggests a certain self-assurance (people on the right side of the map are more likely to have deeply absorbed their mother's rhetorical query, "If all your friends jumped off a bridge, would you do it too?"), but the values on this side of the map do not necessarily indicate a worldview that is more confident or assured than the one on the left side of the map. The right side is, in fact, home to a number of fearful trends, *Apocalyptic Anxiety, Technology Anxiety*, and *Risk Aversion** among them. It is true in general, however, that those Canadians whose values place them at the right side of the map are likely to evaluate ideas and experiences based on their own beliefs, expectations, and even prejudices rather than according to standards that their friends, family, or society at large may hold.

It is not surprising that the trend *Fulfillment Through Work** is found on this side of the map: if these Canadians are successful in their professional lives, it's not because they're striving to impress others; they're working for their own stimulation and fulfillment. *Hyper-Rationality,** a trend that indicates a desire to trust in reason above all else, is also illustrative of the inner direction of the map's right side. The Canadians on this side of the map are likely to make their decisions according to their own logic—not in lockstep with those based on Uncle Max's advice, peer pressure, social convention, or the dictates of an institutional authority. *Importance of Price** is another telling trend in this inner-directed mapspace: Canadians on this side of the map don't much care whether others admire the logos on their

---

* This trend is tracked only in Canada. It and all other asterisked items that follow are defined and appended at the end of this appendix.

sneakers or their cars; just give them something that does the job it's supposed to. People lower down the map on the right-hand side generally have more disposable income than those at the top. They spend a lot, and will pay more for perceived value: carefully assessing the resale value of property, the reputation for reliability of an expensive car, the private school with the best program for their child. Their motivation is to acquire value for money based on the best available information rather than to spend frivolously (lower left) or to impress others (upper left).

At the left of the map, by contrast, we find the values of people who are extremely concerned with what others think. Here we find outer-directed values such as *Ostentatious Consumption, Importance of Physical Beauty,** and *Need for Status Recognition.* Canadians on the left-hand side of the map are more likely than those on the right side to have their behaviour and consumption swayed by social expectations, and to allow their goals to be influenced by those around them. The *Pursuit of Originality** we find on this side of the map is not a deep quest for existential freedom; it suggests, rather, a desire to better elicit the admiration of the crowd by standing slightly apart in some way. Those Canadians who are strong on the trend *Pursuit of Originality* agree with statements such as "I am prepared to pay more for products that are a bit different from those one sees all over" and "I like the small details of my appearance and behaviour to make me stand out from others in a group." These statements exhibit exactly the kind of status-seeking that is one of the key characteristics of this region of the map.

Status-seeking is not the whole story of the left side of the map, however. The outer-directed end of our horizontal axis is also home to some trends that indicate social engagement and social curiosity. The important thing to keep in mind is that these people place a high premium on others' standards and opinions, and whether that attitude results in more superficial efforts to impress (as with *Ostentatious Consumption*) or in a deeper interest in others' perspectives and experiences (as with *Introspection and Empathy*) depends largely on the map's north–south axis.

The vertical axis is a values spectrum whose extremes we have labelled "Conformity and Exclusion" (top) and "Ideals and Individualism" (bottom). It will strike many that the north–south axis contains echoes of the east–west axis. One area of the top of the map exhibits an orientation to conformity and a willingness to defer to external codes and rules; these tendencies may call to mind the outer-directed values we've just explored at the leftmost extreme of the map.

The salient difference between these two extremes of the map (left and top) is that the uppermost extreme exhibits a belief in traditional categories of identity (ethnic, national, gendered, familial) and a desire to belong socially by paying strict attention to the boundaries of those categories, while the leftmost extreme of the map is more focused on achieving social belonging through status-seeking: ostentatious consumption, personal achievement, externally measured success. We might say that, in general, those on the left side of the map tend to focus on acquired status (wealth and achievement) whereas those at the top of the map tend to focus on inherent qualities (ethnicity, gender, inherited position in the hierarchy). In sociology, the difference is referred to as achieved versus ascribed status. At the top of the map, we find the trends *Importance of National Superiority** and *Ethnic Intolerance.** These indicate that Canadians in this socio-cultural region tend to place strong emphasis on being members of well-defined in-groups, and in turn tend to exclude and even exhibit hostility toward others who don't share their particular set of "memberships."

This mental posture does not exist across the entire top region of the socio-cultural map, however. It predominates on the left-hand side of the upper region, but as we move eastward on the map, we begin to encounter trends such as *Anomie and Aimlessness* and *Attraction to Violence,** which register a distinct lack of social connectedness and belonging. Those on the right side of the Conformity and Exclusion zone of the map can find no place for themselves in the achieved hierarchies of status valued on the left side of the map and, unlike Canadians at the bottom of the socio-cultural map, have not found a way to construct their own matrices of meaning and esteem.

The outlook at the bottom of the map, whose lower limit we have labelled "Ideals and Individualism," betrays a more liberal view of life. Canadians in this region are willing to question the categories of identity that are perceived so rigidly farther up the map. Here at the bottom we find trends such as *Flexible Families* and *Flexible Gender Identity* as well as *Cultural Fusion,** *Openness Toward Others,** and *Gender Parity.* The values at the bottom of the map ("You should be able to have what I want for me") clearly incline more toward openness and inclusivity than those at the top.

The individualistic trends in this region, such as *Need for Autonomy,** *Control of Destiny,** and *Rejection of Authority,* facilitate the more idealistic trends. Those Canadians whose values place them at the bottom of this map want to be free to choose their own path in life and to construct their own identity without being constrained by expectations traditionally attached to their gender, nationality, or ethnicity. Because their individualism insists that they not be beholden to whatever group memberships they may happen to hold, these Canadians are unlikely to discriminate against others based on those same categories.

This is a set of values that says, "I am more than the sum of my demographic characteristics; I am open to the challenge and complexity of building or rebuilding an identity from the ground up (including those parts of my background I find meaningful, setting the rest aside)." This attitude engenders a cosmopolitan outlook, hence the placement of the values *Belonging to the Global Village** and *Global Ecological Awareness** here at the bottom of the map.

Now that we've seen how the dimensions of the map operate, we can take a look at how they interact with one another by briefly examining each of the four quadrants of the Canadian map, as we did with the U.S. map in Chapter One. Once again, these quadrants are large spaces encompassing a great number of trends (which in turn encompass many individual questions). No single Canadian's system of values can be fully captured by any of the four regions of the map. The quadrants do, however, give us an understanding of the psychographic territory in which individual

Canadians' values actually exist. We sometimes refer to the quadrants as "macro mental postures"; they offer large, fairly coherent pictures of the four basic kinds of social values perspectives that exist among Canadians.

**The Canadian Socio-Cultural Map:
Mental Postures of the Quadrants**

In the upper-right quadrant we find a set of values emphasizing **Security, Stability, and Exclusion**. The values in this quadrant are, collectively, the harshest on our map. The trend *Social Darwinism** suggests that Canadians in this quadrant see society as a jungle in which competition is fierce and individuals must struggle (sometimes ruthlessly) to survive and/or get ahead. These Canadians are likely to feel disconnected from society *(Anomie and Aimlessness)*, and are also inclined to be uneasy about changes unfolding around them, hence the trends *Technology Anxiety, Aversion to Complexity,* and even *Apocalyptic Anxiety.**

The Security, Stability, and Exclusion Quadrant

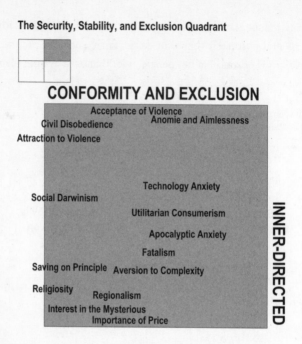

CONFORMITY AND EXCLUSION

This is a quadrant made volatile by its fear. On one hand, anxiety about a changing world gives rise to this quadrant's security-seeking bent: trends like *Saving on Principle, Religiosity,* and *Regionalism** suggest that these Canadians are looking for safe havens (financial security, spiritual solace, a sense of tribal or local belonging) to shelter them from what they see as the chaos of the world at large. On the other hand, the same fears that inspire this longing for order can also lead to intense frustration capable of erupting into violence. Hence the appearance in this quadrant of trends such as *Acceptance of Violence* (violence in everyday life is normal and can be both cathartic and effective) and *Civil Disobedience*.*[1]

Clearly, the Canadians whose values place them in this quadrant are not the winners in our society. They find themselves caught in a cycle of

---

1. The trend *Civil Disobedience* does not denote an idealistic resistance of power; rather it is more a selfish renunciation of the rule of law. Respondents strong on *Civil Disobedience* agreed with statements such as, "When you think a law is stupid, it's okay not to obey it" and "Governments are going too far: it's okay to cheat on your taxes, just don't get caught."

fearfulness and hostility toward the world around them. They are on the lookout for those they can blame for their own misfortunes by voting, if they can be motivated, for right-wing parties that promise to punish the real culprits: teachers' unions, welfare cheats, and illegal immigrants. Their sense of *Fatalism* (the belief that one can't do much to affect the course of one's life) and *Anomie and Aimlessness* (the sense that one doesn't have strong aspirations or any clear direction in life) are also telling indications of the bleakness of the worldview we find in this quadrant.

Moving on now to the lower-right quadrant, the region we've labelled the **Autonomy and Well-Being** quadrant, we find, in stark contrast with the segment just described, an extremely postmodern psychographic space. This quadrant combines the self-directed attitude of the right side of the map with the autonomy and social engagement of the map's lower extreme. In this quadrant we find a strong rejection of traditional rules and forms of authority, evidenced by the trends *Rejection of Authority, Control of Destiny,** and *Rejection of Order*.

The Autonomy and Well-Being Quadrant

Pursuit of Happiness to the Detriment of Duty
Community Involvement
Skepticism Toward Small Business
Hyper-Rationality
Deconsumption
Risk Aversion
Spiritual Quest
Need for Escape
Heterarchy   Everyday Ethics
Rejection of Order
Equal Relationship with Youth

Fulfillment Through Work
Importance of Spontaneity
Rejection of Authority
Global Ecological Awareness
New Social Responsiblity
Control of Destiny

INNER-DIRECTED

IDEALS AND INDIVIDUALISM

Despite the strong individualist bent of this quadrant, we find no excess of selfishness. The lower-right region of the map does contain the trend *Pursuit of Happiness to the Detriment of Duty** (meaning respondents disagreed with statements such as "It is important to fulfill your duties and obligations to others before pursuing your personal pleasure"), but that trend coexists with *Community Involvement,** *Everyday Ethics, Global Ecological Awareness,** and *New Social Responsibility.** They are saying: act responsibly to your parents, children, the community, but not out of duty, guilt, or noblesse oblige; do it because in your heart or in your long-term self-interest you know it's the right or smart thing to do.

Although they are committed to autonomy and are thus unwilling to adhere to anyone else's vision of "the good life," the Canadians whose values place them in this quadrant are certainly not without standards of right and wrong. They are likely to construct their own systems of ethics and sets of rules based on principles they find compelling, rather than holding to codes of conduct handed down from a religious leader or family patriarch. Their belief in the *Pursuit of Happiness to the Detriment of Duty,** for example, given that it exists alongside the other decidedly unselfish trends listed above, likely indicates that these Canadians do not organize their behaviour in a duty versus personal happiness binary. Rather, community involvement, social responsibility, and personal ethics are all part of the balance (a balance that also includes hedonism) that *leads* to happiness and fulfillment.

The trends *Deconsumption** and *Skepticism Toward Big Business** suggest that Canadians in this quadrant are not trying to find happiness in keeping up with the Joneses or obeying the dictates of advertisers; rather, consistent with their position at the inner-directed end of the map, they're seeking fulfillment by exploiting their own resources: in a personal *Spiritual Quest,* in taking advantage of day-to-day pleasures *(Importance of Spontaneity),* and in occasional personal retreat via travel, relaxation, or a cup of cappuccino *(Need for Escape*).*

This quadrant is where we find what we call the defining segment of the Baby Boomer cohort: the Autonomous Rebels. These are the Canadians who rebelled during the 60s, indulged during the 70s, ascended professionally during the 80s, and have since remained an extremely powerful force in Canadian society, occupying important positions in business and government. It is not only the Boomers' numbers, but also the strength of their vision and the legal reforms (such as the 1982 Charter of Rights and Freedoms) they enthusiastically embraced that have made them such a powerful cultural force in Canadian society. Their early questioning of deference to the authority of traditional hierarchical institutions—the father in the family, the priest in the parish, the teacher in the classroom—has been expressed in adulthood by the questioning of Canada's traditional political elites and later the leadership of large corporate enterprises both public and private, national and global. Their embracing of the value *Heterarchy* reflects their egalitarian idealism for the ideal governance model of all organizations, from the family to the multinational corporation. To them there is no one set of a few permanent leaders with the vast majority relegated to a permanent class of followers. Rather they see a more fluid style of leadership whereby someone leads one day and follows the next. Information in this context replaces ideology as the basis for organizing human activity.

In the lower-left, **Openness and Experience** quadrant, we find those who share the lower-right quadrant's emphasis on personal autonomy and progressive values, but are more outer-directed, taking greater interest in the perspectives and judgments of people around them. This quadrant's rejection of traditional forms of authority is manifested in trends such as *Need for Autonomy,** *Flexibility of Gender Identity,** *Flexible Definition of Family,** and *Gender Parity.*

The Openness and Experience Quadrant

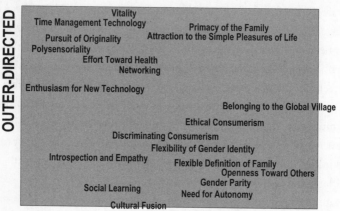

IDEALS AND INDIVIDUALISM

These Canadians, like those in the Autonomy and Well-Being quadrant, want the freedom to define their own lifestyles and identities and don't wish to be beholden to the prescriptions and proscriptions of religion, patriarchy, or traditional codes of propriety. Here again we find idealism, but this idealism is of a more communitarian sort, placing greater emphasis on social connectedness than the lower-right quadrant does. For example, we find the trends *Cultural Fusion,** *Social Learning,** *Openness Toward Others,** and *Introspection and Empathy* in this quadrant. These trends all indicate a desire to learn from and be enriched by people different from oneself, and a belief that different cultural groups can live together harmoniously in a single interdependent society.

The interpersonal connectedness of this lower-left quadrant also manifests itself in trends such as *Networking* and *Primacy of the Family*. The former suggests that Canadians in this region of the map are interested in using their links with others to help them learn and be successful in their professional and personal lives. The latter suggests that these Canadians' families—which, in addition to traditional nuclear families, include blended families and common-law and same-sex relationships—are central to their daily lives and to the way they understand themselves in relation to the world around them.

We also find strong experience-seeking and personal development strains in this quadrant, especially in the area nearest the leftmost extreme of the map. This quadrant's interest in novelty, progress, and originality is manifested in trends such as *Enthusiasm for New Technology, Pursuit of Originality,** and *Polysensoriality.** These trends all indicate an interest in the consumption of new, unusual products that impress in some way: they may be sophisticated gadgets, remarkable for their portability and usefulness, or familiar products with a stylish twist that makes them stand out, like the multicoloured iMac. There is a certain element of status-seeking in these especially outer-directed trends, but nearby (and therefore correlated) trends such as *Discriminating Consumerism, Ethical Consumerism,* and *Attraction to the Simple Pleasures of Life** suggest that this quadrant's consumption and hedonism are fairly thoughtful and discerning.

The combination of *Networking* and *Enthusiasm for New Technology* also explains this quadrant being the home of the early adopters of new information and entertainment technology. These people are wired to their like-minded peers in Canada and elsewhere on the planet who share their values and interests.

Personal development–oriented trends in this quadrant, like the experience- and novelty-seeking ones, indicate a certain amount of status-seeking, tempered by a commitment to autonomy and self-fulfillment. The trends *Effort Toward Health, Vitality,* and *Time Management Technology** all indicate a drive to self-improvement of a kind that can be both satisfactory to the person achieving it and impressive to others. Given this quadrant's outer-directedness, it is fairly predictable that this penchant for personal development is motivated at least in part by a desire to impress others; but the quadrant's proximity to the bottom of the map (that is, its autonomy) suggests that these Canadians aren't likely to try to impress anyone with achievements toward which they do not feel personally inclined in the first place; for example, the sculpted bodies or cool cars of those in the quadrant above, to which we now turn our attention.

The final, upper-left quadrant is underpinned by **Social Success, Materialism, and Pride**. In this quadrant we again encounter the penchant for status-seeking we glimpsed in the lower-left quadrant, but here it is not tempered by the autonomy of the bottom of the map. In this quadrant, achieving the esteem of one's peers and associates in a variety of departments is paramount: here we find *Ostentatious Consumption, Concern for Appearance, Need for Status Recognition,* and *Need for Personal Achievement.**

The Social Success, Materialism, and Pride Quadrant

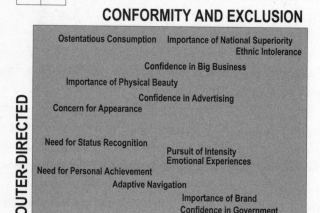

The status that those in this quadrant desire (or wish to protect) is not only socio-economic (as manifested through their conspicuous consumption), but also ascribed status such as ethnicity and nationality, hence the placement of the trends *Importance of National Superiority** and *Ethnic Intolerance** in this quadrant. Canadians whose values place them in this quadrant are likely to believe in many traditional distinctions among people—especially distinctions of race, religion, and class. The mental posture we find in this quadrant is one that was largely formed when phrases like "being from the wrong side of the tracks" meant something to most Canadians.

In her sparely wrought stories of life in rural southwestern Ontario, Alice Munro frequently conjures a time when this mental posture was dominant in Canada. An example drawn from a memoir Munro published in *The New Yorker* in summer of 2002: "Perhaps my mother would have found a way to tell me that once you went into certain houses as an equal and a friend—and this was true even if they were on some level perfectly respectable houses—you showed that the value you put on yourself was not very high, and after that others would value you accordingly. I would have argued with her, of course, and the more fiercely because I would have known that what she was saying was true."

This quadrant's attachment to order, which derives from its placement at the top of the map, does not manifest itself in the same ways as that of the upper-right quadrant, but it is certainly present. Not only is it revealed in the quadrant's attachment to the (in more modern Canadians' minds antiquated) social divisions just described; it also shows itself in the quadrant's deferential tendencies. Here we find the trends *Confidence in Big Business, Confidence in Advertising,* and *Confidence in Government.** These Canadians aren't averse to being told what to do, provided the entities giving orders are venerable and trusted: government, large corporations, and religious institutions. They came of age in a society in which pastors, business leaders, and political figures were thought of as exemplary citizens in every respect. These people were our betters to whom deference was due, like the captains of industry who appeared on the covers of business magazines staring out from behind their tidy desks, ties neatly tied, glasses straight and gleaming, projecting an image of stolidity and reliability. The Prime Minister of Canada was a figure deserving of respect such as Jean Chrétien could only dream in 2002 as he polished the rearview mirror he had installed for security purposes on his desk in the House of Commons.

One of the key differences between those at the top and the bottom of the map is an orientation to hierarchy. Those at the top believe that the pyramid is the natural metaphor for the ordering of society and the institutions in it. A few or even one at the top lead, and growing numbers toward the bottom follow. Those at the left side see this as a natural God-given order; those on the right the law of the jungle. This hierarchy applies as much to the ordering of such social institutions as the family, the church, the workplace, and the military as to the consumer marketplace with its hierarchy of symbolically evocative products, services, and experiences. *Heterarchy* describes the mental posture of those at the bottom of the map, where we all lead and follow depending on our interest, skills, and time available to do the job, not our permanent place in the status hierarchy.

The evolution of the Canadian population from 1983 to 2001 is graphically portrayed in Figures F6 and F7, respectively, which show the average position of the population as measured by CROP's annual survey of Canadian social values. As I discussed in Chapter Five, during the first period (1983 to 1996), Canadians moved down and right on the map—from the Social Success, Materialism, and Pride quadrant into the Autonomy and Well-Being quadrant. The proportion of Canadians having values in the bottom third of the map, at the Ideals and Individualism end of the north–south axis, rose from 25 per cent to 44 per cent.

F6

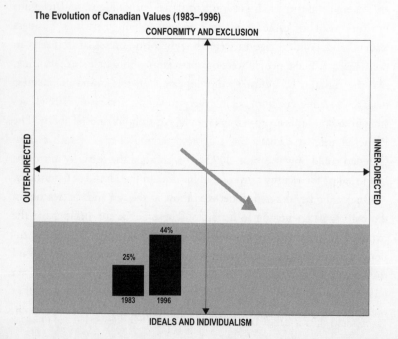

The Evolution of Canadian Values (1983–1996)

In the 1996–2001 period, however, the Canadian population regressed—moving up and right toward the Security, Stability, and Exclusion quadrant, with the proportion in the lower third of the map declining from 44 per cent to 28 per cent.

F7

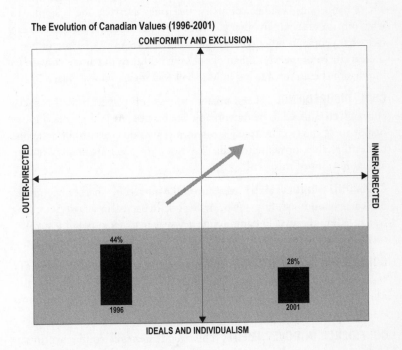

The Evolution of Canadian Values (1996-2001)

VALUES TRACKED ONLY IN CANADA

APOCALYPTIC ANXIETY Tendency to believe that the world is heading toward major upheavals in the future, and to anticipate these changes with anxiety.

ATTRACTION TO THE SIMPLE PLEASURES OF LIFE Taking great pleasure in accomplishing simple household tasks, such as gardening or fixing things, that others might find trivial. These types of tasks take on a symbolic value in that they offer people some respite from feeling that they're racing against the clock, while responding to their need for self-expression through the accomplishment of something simple but pleasant.

ATTRACTION TO VIOLENCE   Feeling an attraction to violence. Taking pleasure not only in watching violent movies and TV programs but also from the rush derived from violent emotions within. People strongest on this trend seek intense experiences that let them feel and share strong emotions, and many feel aimless. Feeling somewhat excluded, they tend to contravene laws and regulations to achieve their goals.

BELONGING TO THE GLOBAL VILLAGE   Impression of being "plugged into" what's happening in other countries; that one's everyday life is similar to what others experience in other parts of the world. Also, a sense that one can feel what people in other parts of the world are feeling. A feeling of being more a citizen of the world than of one's own country, of participating in an international culture, of living in Marshall McLuhan's "global village."

CIVIL DISOBEDIENCE   Legitimizing a lack of respect for the social contract, considered to be unworkable in any case. Anything goes if it can help people survive in today's economy. Working or hiring someone under the table, or taking certain liberties with one's income tax return, are expressions of this trend.

COMMUNITY INVOLVEMENT   Measure of the interest in what's happening in one's neighbourhood, city, town, or region. Reflected in activities ranging from reading the weekly community newspaper to socio-political involvement in community organizations. Also an indicator of social conscience.

CONFIDENCE IN ADVERTISING   Tendency to trust and use advertising as a source of reliable information. Also, a tendency to identify with the fashions and the role models promoted by advertising and the consumer society.

CONFIDENCE IN GOVERNMENT   This trend measures confidence in the ability of government to positively affect how society works. Tendency to believe that government performs a socially beneficial function.

CONTROL OF DESTINY   Desire to escape from the domination of society over daily life. The desire to control all aspects of one's life, even those determined by forces over which we seem to have little control. Tendency to believe that not everything is predetermined, that one can influence the course of events.

CULTURAL FUSION   This trend identifies the view that other cultures have a great deal to give us, and measures people's inclination to incorporate some of these cultural influences into their own lives. The meeting and fusion of totally different cultures produces rich and varied microcultures. This phenomenon is already apparent in many areas, such as music *(world beat)* and food *(fusion cuisine)*. Well adapted to the complexity of the New World Order, people strongest on this trend tend to consider themselves citizens of the global village.

DECONSUMPTION The willingness to adopt a lifestyle in which consumption plays a less dominant role. This attitude is expressed in a desire to limit or reduce one's consumption of goods and to spend less than before.

ETHNIC INTOLERANCE Intolerance toward immigrants and ethnic groups. Considering immigration a threat to the purity of the country, believing that the various ethnic groups should abandon their own customs and culture and adopt our own. People strongest on this trend display conformist values and consider national superiority especially important.

FLEXIBILITY OF GENDER IDENTITY The feeling that one has both a masculine and a feminine side to one's personality. The desire to actively explore and express these different facets of one's personality. Having the feeling of being more masculine at some times and more feminine at others. This tendency is much stronger among women than men.

FLEXIBLE DEFINITION OF FAMILY Willingness to accept non-traditional definitions of "family," such as common-law marriages. The belief that family should be defined by emotional links rather than by legal formalities or institutions. Also, the belief that society should be open to new definitions of what constitutes a family.

FULFILLMENT THROUGH WORK A need to invest one's professional life with meaning and to find personal fulfillment through one's work. Also, a need to feel that one's work is useful to others and has some social value.

GLOBAL ECOLOGICAL AWARENESS Tendency to believe that all the environmental phenomena on earth are interrelated. A systemic vision of environmental events, a conviction that ecological problems in one area of the world can have an impact on distant regions.

HYPER-RATIONALITY A propensity to give priority to reason as the principal way of understanding life. A desire to keep one's emotional life "on an even keel," to use logic and reason to control one's feelings and emotions, and to base day-to-day decisions on reason and logic. A reluctance to experience emotions. (Inverse of *Pursuit of Intensity and Emotional Experiences*.)

IMPORTANCE OF NATIONAL SUPERIORITY Need to prove to others, and to oneself, that one's country is superior to others in many ways. Tendency to see oneself as superior to foreigners.

IMPORTANCE OF PHYSICAL BEAUTY Tendency to place a high priority on a youthful and attractive body, and being willing to make a considerable effort to attain and keep such a bodily appearance.

IMPORTANCE OF PRICE Giving great weight to price as a purchasing criterion. Consumers strong on this trend always take price into account when considering a purchase, even when the product or service is a particularly desired one.

NEED FOR AUTONOMY Need for autonomy in daily life. The desire to exert as much control as possible over all aspects of daily life (work, consumption, etc.).

NEED FOR ESCAPE The desire to regularly escape the stresses and responsibilities of everyday life.

NEED FOR PERSONAL ACHIEVEMENT The drive to achieve personal and social success. Taking on difficult ventures to demonstrate one's ability to succeed.

NEW SOCIAL RESPONSIBILITY A deep feeling of belonging to one's community and a pronounced feeling of social responsibility, where mutual assistance places a key role. This trend is associated with a desire to be open to others, and to better understand the society and the world around us.

OPENNESS TOWARD OTHERS Need for communication and deep, affective exchanges with others. A desire for frank, warm, and spontaneous relations with people.

POLYSENSORIALITY Tendency to give priority to the sensorial perceptions aroused by the non-visual senses. A more sensual, intuitive, and affective approach to life.

PURSUIT OF HAPPINESS TO THE DETRIMENT OF DUTY Motivation to act and live according to one's selfish impulses rather than one's obligations to others. A need to express one's personality and to pursue happiness and pleasure, despite the dictates of duty or morality.

PURSUIT OF ORIGINALITY A need to feel different from others. A preoccupation with demonstrating one's individuality through original touches.

REGIONALISM A closer identification with one's province or region than with one's country. Believing that one's feeling of belonging to a region or province is of greater importance than the identity of being "Canadian."

RISK AVERSION A reluctance to take risks in order to get what one wants. People who are strong on this trend desire security and stability in all areas, including the most mundane aspects of everyday life. This trend also measures conservative buying behaviours. (Inverse of *Penchant for Risk.*)

SKEPTICISM TOWARD BIG BUSINESS   A lack of confidence in the commitment of big-business owners to the provision of quality goods and services, and skepticism toward their motives and ethics. Measures the belief that there is a conflict of interest between the public and business, and that companies are only profit-driven. (Inverse of *Confidence in Big Business.*)

SOCIAL DARWINISM Tendency to believe that society's regulatory mechanisms and rules governing social relations are those of the jungle (the strongest prevail, the weak fall by the wayside, etc.). Tendency to believe that the great socio-democratic ideals of recent years have run their course; that society is in the process of accepting the inevitability of poverty and greater social inequalities. A belief that one must look after one's own needs; that society has no responsibility to help those less fortunate.

SOCIAL LEARNING Attraction to and interest in diversity. Feeling that there is a great deal to learn through contact and conversation with people different from you, who come from other backgrounds and places. Diversity is perceived as a source of personal enrichment, a way to satisfy a hunger for discovery and exploration and to extend a network of contacts. This trend is also associated with a respect for other people and cultures, as well as a heightened social conscience.

TIME MANAGEMENT TECHNOLOGY Openness to technology that helps us to manage our time. For example, a strong interest in and/or use of such electronic time-saving devices as microwave ovens, video-cassette recorders, automatic banking machines, and answering machines. Using these devices, not only to save time, but to give oneself more control over the timing of one's activities.

FIND YOUR QUADRANT

If we haven't yet surveyed you in one of our studies to diagnose your social values, here is your chance to find out how you would likely be placed on our social values map. Please visit our Web site at www.environics.net and follow the links to the Social Values page for *Fire and Ice*. There, you will find a short version of the more extensive social values questionnaire that we field to Canadians annually and to Americans every four years. Just fill it out and submit it and we will calculate a general position for you on the map described in this book. We will also characterize generally the social values and mental postures of people in the quadrant you fall into on the North American map.

While you're visiting our Web site, you might also stop to see which of the thirteen Canadian social values "tribes" you are most likely to be a member of. These tribes are the subject of my other books on social values, *Sex in the Snow* and *Better Happy Than Rich?* The various tribes emerged from our statistical analysis of how people are grouped based on the similarity of their social values. Not everyone is clearly a member of one and only one tribe, and given that we can't ask you our whole battery of several hundred items, we will give you a result that indicates, with about a 70 per cent chance of being correct, the most likely tribe (or tribes) of which you are a member within your age cohort (Youth, Baby Boomers, Elders). For your Canadian tribal diagnosis, just click on the links to the Social Values questionnaire for *Sex in the Snow* or *Better Happy Than Rich?* fill it out, and have fun. If you're an American reader of this book, you can still participate, but you'll have to suffer the small humiliation of being classified as a member of a Canadian social values tribe.

Just remember: answer honestly and directly to get the best estimate of your placement on the maps and of your tribal affiliation; there are no right or wrong answers to questions about your worldviews, orientations, and values!

BIBLIOGRAPHY

"America's New Utopias." *The Economist,* 30 August 2001.

Adams, Michael. *Better Happy Than Rich? Canadians, Money, and the Meaning of Life.* Toronto: Penguin Books, 2000.

Adams, Michael. *Sex in the Snow.* Toronto: Penguin Books, 1997.

Block, Richard. *Firearms in Canada and Eight Other Western Countries: Selected Findings of the 1996 International Crime (Victim) Survey.* Ottawa: Department of Justice, Canadian Firearms Centre, 1997.

Brooks, David. *Bobos in Paradise.* Toronto: Simon and Schuster, 2000.

Brooks, David. "One Nation, Slightly Divisible." *The Atlantic Monthly,* December 2001.

Clarkson, Stephen. *Uncle Sam and US: Globalization, Neoconservatism, and the Canadian State.* Toronto: University of Toronto Press Inc., 2002.

Frum, David. *How We Got Here: The 70's.* Toronto: Random House Inc., 2000.

Gladwell, Malcolm. "Designs for Working." *The New Yorker,* 11 December 2000.

Garreau, Joel. *The Nine Nations of North America.* New York: Avon, 1981.

Gwyn, Richard. *The 49th Paradox: Canada in North America.* Toronto: McClelland & Stewart Ltd., 1985.

Himmelfarb, Gertrude. *One Nation, Two Cultures.* New York: Vintage, 2001.

Hurtig, Mel. *The Vanishing Country: Is It Too Late to Save Canada?* Toronto: McClelland & Stewart Ltd., 2002.

Inglehart, Ronald. *Modernization and Postmodernization*. Princeton: Princeton University Press, 1997.

"Less Fun, Less Sleep, More Work: An American Portrait." *Report from the National Sleep Foundation,* 27 March 2001.

Lind, Michael. "The Beige and the Black." *New York Times Magazine,* 16 August 1998.

Lipset, Seymour Martin. *American Exceptionalism*. New York: W.W. Norton, 1996.

Lipset, Seymour Martin. *Continental Divide*. Toronto: C.D. Howe Institute, 1989.

Lester, Toby. "Oh, Gods." *The Atlantic Monthly,* February 2002.

Martinez, Michael D. "Turning Out or Tuning Out? Electoral Participation in Canada and the United States." *Canada and the United States: Differences That Count*. Broadview Press Ltd., 2000.

Munro, Alice. "Lying Under the Apple Tree." *The New Yorker,* 17 & 24 June 2002.

Murphy, Brian, and Michael Wolfson. "Income Inequality in North America: Does the 49th Parallel Still Matter?" *The Canadian Economic Observer,* August 2000.

Newman, Peter C. *The Canadian Revolution*. Toronto: Penguin Books, 1996.

Nevitte, Neil. *The Decline of Deference*. Peterborough: Broadview Press, 1996.

Osberg, Lars. "Time, Money and Inequality in International Perspective," International Labour Organization, 28 November 2002.

Phillips, Kevin. *Wealth and Democracy: A Political History of the American Rich*. New York: Broadway Books, 2002.

Putnam, Robert D. *Bowling Alone*. Toronto: Simon and Schuster, 2000.

Ray, Paul. *Cultural Creatives*. New York: Three Rivers Press, 2001.

Riesman, David, Nathan Glazer, and Reuel Denney. *The Lonely Crowd: A Study of the Changing American Character*. New Haven: Yale University Press, 2001.

Rokeach, Milton. *The Nature of Human Values*. New York: Free Press, 1973.

Slouka, Mark. "A Year Later." *Harper's Magazine*, September 2002.

Simpson, Jeffrey. *Star-Spangled Canadians*. Toronto: HarperCollins Publishers Ltd., 2000.

Stark, Rodney. *A Theory of Religion*. New York: P. Lang, 1987.

Thomas, David M. *Canada and the United States: Differences That Count* (2nd ed.). Peterborough: Broadview Press, 2000.

de Tocqueville, Alexis. *Democracy in America*. Ed. J.P. Mayer. Trans. George Lawrence. New York: Harper & Row, 1966.

United States (U.S.) Bureau of the Census. *Statistical Abstract of the United States, 2001*. Washington, D.C.: U.S. Government Printing Office, 2001.

Veblen, Thorstein. *The Theory of the Leisure Class: An Economic Study of Institutions*. New York: Macmillan, 1902.

Wolfe, Alan. *One Nation, After All*. New York: Penguin, 1998.

Yankelovich, Daniel. *New Rules*. New York: Random House Inc., 1981.

INDEX